This collection of simple to use and [illegible] jumpstart pupils' understanding of the historical skills [illegible]gy, enquiry, historical inference, and knowledge and understan[illegible] of people, places and time.

Uncovering history is an effective way to engage pupils in a topic and can act as a fantastic hook for learning. This book will enable you to make history a fundamental part of your classroom, to enhance not only the pupils' historical understanding but also to deepen their understanding in other subjects.

Areas covered include:

- Stone Age, Bronze Age and Iron Age
- Egyptians and Ancient Greeks
- Romans
- Saxons, Vikings and Normans
- Tudors and Stuarts
- Victorians
- World War II and post-war Britain
- Local history.

This indispensable classroom resource will celebrate history and give children the opportunity to experience the thrill of finding out about the past. It will be a lifeline to any classroom teacher looking to teach history in a fun and exciting way.

Sarah Whitehouse has worked in the primary classroom for a decade and was the first teacher in Wales to be awarded the Gold Quality Mark for geography for her school. She has a number of publications specialising in primary history and geography and is currently PGCE Primary Programme Leader for Primary and Early Years (Humanities Specialist) at the University of the West of England in Bristol.

Karan Vickers-Hulse has been a primary school teacher for 15 years, most recently as a Deputy Head. She has written a number of publications for KCP Publications and is currently Senior Lecturer in Primary English and Undergraduate Programme Leader for Primary and Early Years at the University of the West of England in Bristol.

Jumpstart!

Jumpstart! History
Engaging activities for ages 7–12
Sarah Whitehouse and Karan Vickers-Hulse

Jumpstart! Geography
Engaging activities for ages 7–12
Mark Jones and Sarah Whitehouse

Jumpstart! Thinking Skills and Problem Solving
Games and activities for ages 7–14
Steve Bowkett

Jumpstart! Maths (2nd Edition)
Maths activities and games for ages 5–14
John Taylor

Jumpstart! Grammar
Games and activities for ages 7–14
Pie Corbett and Julia Strong

Jumpstart! Spanish and Italian
Engaging activities for ages 7–12
Catherine Watts and Hilary Phillips

Jumpstart! French and German
Engaging activities for ages 7–12
Catherine Watts and Hilary Phillips

Jumpstart! Drama
Games and activities for ages 5–11
Teresa Cremin, Roger McDonald, Emma Goff and Louise Blakemore

Jumpstart! Science
Games and activities for ages 5–11
Rosemary Feasey

Jumpstart! Storymaking
Games and activities for ages 7–12
Pie Corbett

Jumpstart! Poetry
Games and activities for ages 7–12
Pie Corbett

Jumpstart! Creativity
Games and activities for ages 7–14
Steve Bowkett

Jumpstart! ICT
ICT activities and games for ages 7–14
John Taylor

Jumpstart! Numeracy
Maths activities and games for ages 5–14
John Taylor

Jumpstart! Literacy
Key Stage 2/3 literacy games
Pie Corbett

JUMPSTART! HISTORY

ENGAGING ACTIVITIES FOR AGES 7–12

Sarah Whitehouse and
Karan Vickers-Hulse

LONDON AND NEW YORK

First published 2015
by Routledge
2 Park Square, Milton Park, Abingdon, Oxon OX14 4RN

and by Routledge
711 Third Avenue, New York, NY 10017

Routledge is an imprint of the Taylor & Francis Group, an informa business

British Library Cataloguing in Publication Data
A catalogue record for this book is available from the British Library

Library of Congress Cataloging in Publication Data
Whitehouse, Sarah.
Jumpstart! history : engaging activities for ages 7–12 / Sarah Whitehouse, Karan Vickers-Hulse.
pages cm. — (Jumpstart!)
1. History—Study and teaching (Elementary)--Activity programs.
2. History—Study and teaching (Middle school)—Activity programs.
I. Vickers-Hulse, Karan. II. Title.
LB1581.W45 2014
372.89—dc23
2014017058

ISBN: 978-0-415-72901-7 (hbk)
ISBN: 978-0-415-72902-4 (pbk)
ISBN: 978-1-315-85135-8 (ebk)

Typeset in Palatino and Scala Sans
by FiSH Books Ltd, Enfield

Printed and bound in Great Britain by
TJ International Ltd, Padstow, Cornwall

Contents

Authors' note

The periods of history covered in this book are vast and span thousands, often millions, of years. Although we would like to include all the key events from each period this has not been possible, therefore we have selected some significant events, people and places and provided activities to explore these further.

Every effort has been made to ensure that facts, information and dates are accurate; however, history is always open to interpretation and slight variations from other sources may be evident.

ACKNOWLEDGEMENTS

We are very grateful to the many teachers, students, children and colleagues that we have learnt with and from.

Introduction

Jumpstart! History provides a wealth of ideas for learning history through games and activities.

The book is divided up into eight themed chapters, which look at periods of history in chronological order. Each chapter includes key historical skills such as enquiry, chronology and knowledge and understanding. In the introduction to each chapter there is an overview of the period providing some key historical subject knowledge. We would suggest that the introductions are particularly helpful for those readers wanting to be clear about how this period of time is connected to other periods and as a starting point for subject knowledge acquisition. Each chapter is divided into sections which include a little bit of knowledge and then a number of activities.

We hope that this book provides a way into history and supports teachers and parents by providing quick and ready ideas to help children to develop an understanding of the past. The activities provided in this book can be used to:

- introduce a new theme or topic
- establish what somebody already knows
- form part of a lesson beginning, middle or ending
- provide an extension activity.

CHAPTER 1

Stone Age, Bronze Age and Iron Age

This chapter aims to give an overview of what life was like thousands of years ago providing opportunities for the children to make enquiries about how the lives of Stone Age, Bronze Age and Iron Age people were different to their lives today.

The Stone Age went on for a long time but life did not change all that much during that period, priorities were: gathering food and surviving the elements. It was named The Stone Age as tools and weapons were made of stone. Later came the Bronze Age because people started to use bronze for decoration, tools, armour, weapons and building materials.

Millions of years ago, periods of time were named not after the civilisations but after the tools that were used; hence the Stone Age, Bronze Age and Iron Age.

WHAT WAS IT LIKE IN THE STONE AGE?

A little bit of knowledge . . .

The Stone Age lasted more than 3 million years and ended in around 2500BCE with the introduction of metal tools and weaponry.

It is thought that the first British settlers came from Europe around 500,000 years ago and could walk across the land mass that joined Britain to Europe at that time. Britain only became separated from Europe approximately 8500 years ago when the melting ice formed the English Channel.

In the Stone Age life revolved around gathering food in often harsh conditions and surviving – Stone Age people would sometimes shelter in caves for protection. Later in the Stone Age people discovered farming and began to work the land in a more structured way.

What is a henge?

The first farmers in the latter part of the Stone Age began building a series of major monuments. During this time there were many mounds and monuments built as burial sites or worship structures. The word henge refers to a type of mound that was built in the Neolithic period (4200BCE–2500BCE) in the later part of the Stone Age. There were more than 400 henges built, many of which are still standing today; the most famous being Stonehenge in Wiltshire. There are many other surviving henges including examples at Avebury and The Ring of Brodgar in Orkney.

Activities

1. ***Stonehenge structures***

Look at images of stone circles that were made in Stone Age times such as Stonehenge, Stanton Drew and the Nine Maidens of Boskednan and ask children to think about what they believe the purpose of these structures were (e.g. measure the movement of the sun and moon, as a special place of worship); providing reasons for their thoughts. Talk about how historians believe these structures may have been used, for example: the summer solstice was very important to people in the past because they needed the sun to stay alive to produce their crops and it was a time of celebration. The stone circles often line up with the rising of the sun and therefore some people believe that this meant that the Stone Age people may have worshipped the sun.

2. ***Stonehenge: What does it mean to you?***

Although Stonehenge was built over 5000 years ago it is still a site of significance today for a number of reasons: an iconic British monument, a place of worship and somewhere to feel at peace or a symbol of the past. Show children paintings of Stonehenge by the famous artists Constable and Turner and ask them to think about why these artists chose to paint Stonehenge. Why does

Stonehenge draw so many people to it? Ask children to make a poster, pamphlet or leaflet to encourage tourists to Stonehenge – they can draw their interpretation of Stonehenge and include information from reputable websites.

What can we learn from Skara Brae?

Skara Brae is a New Stone Age (Neolithic) settlement located in the Orkney Islands in Scotland. The site was originally built around an old 'midden' site which consisted of human waste such as food remains, excrement and animal bones. It is made up of eight houses set in a cluster and is one of the most complete Neolithic villages in Europe. The design of the village was very sophisticated and this tells us much about the changes in the Stone Age from beginning to the end. By the Neolithic period the Stone Age people had developed the skills and competence to improve their quality of life. The village had features such as sunken houses to protect from the weather; square rooms with a hearth for heating and cooking; stone built pieces of furniture such as cupboards and seats; a door made from a stone slab that could be opened and closed and a drainage system for a basic form of toilet.

Activity

Escape to the Orkneys

Ask children to imagine they are estate agents and have been given the task of selling a home in Skara Brae to a Neolithic family who are looking to settle. (Remember to point out to children that this would not have been how people found settlements in Neolithic times!) Children should sell the features of the house and use persuasive language to entice their buyers. This works as a written exercise or it can be done as a drama activity.

How did life change in the Stone Age?

The Stone Age spanned many thousands of years and can be broadly divided into three periods.

	Stone Tools	Homes	Sites of Significance
Palaeolithic (Old Stone Age)	Stone tools used	People were nomadic and did not settle in one place. They were hunter-gatherers	No recorded sites of significance
Mesolithic (Middle Stone Age)	Stone tools used and developed – smaller and more effective	People were still nomadic but often settled for longer periods in temporary camps	No recorded sites of significance
Neolithic (New Stone Age)	Stone tools becoming more sophisticated First evidence of pottery	People began to settle on farms and create permanent settlements	First recorded evidence of sites such as henges

Throughout the Stone Age there was no written language and it was not so easy to communicate. This is why it is much harder for historians to gather evidence from this period; one way they can find out about the lives of Stone Age people is by looking at cave paintings which the Stone Age people used to represent their daily lives.

Activities

1. *Cave stories: picture this*

Before written language the Stone Age people used paintings to tell stories. Put the children into groups and ask one person to be the 'cave artist'. They are to pick a message from a pile and draw it for the rest of the group to guess. This will help the children to understand how difficult it must have been to share and preserve stories with no written language.

Suggested messages:

I have caught a fish in the river
I have killed a deer for dinner
It is raining and cold – I need to find shelter
As soon as the sun rises we are on the move
I will use my cutting stone to make a weapon
I will use these stones to make fire
Today, we... (children to draw pictures of what they would have done in Stone Age)

2. *Cave paintings*

Look at some examples of cave paintings and give children the following enquiry questions to discuss in groups:

- What does this painting show?
- What does it tell us about their lives?
- Why do you think they chose to draw this?
- How reliable do you think these paintings are as a source of evidence?

Now ask children to make their own cave paintings. Find a space outside that can be the 'cave wall' – this can be a real wall or you can create a wall by pinning large pieces of card to a surface and covering it with PVA glue and sand; this will provide a rough surface as a canvas. Ask children to collect items from the environment to paint with (Stone Age people did not have any paintbrushes); they can use sticks, stones, leaves and anything else that is natural in their environment – they could even use their fingers. Cave paintings normally comprised deer, animals and simple patterns. They rarely drew figures (this came in later paintings) although handprints were a common feature.

What tools did Stone Age people use?

Stone Age people relied on the environment around them to provide their resources. They used stone to make their weapons and tools; becoming more sophisticated as they moved from Palaeolithic to Neolithic. Flint was readily available and although it is a hard stone it chips easily creating sharp edges that can be modified for a variety of purposes. The Stone Age people spent a lot of time creating suitable tools that were fit for purpose, for example: using a round pebble to smooth and snap large flint stones into cutting tools and scrapers.

Activities

1. Using Stone Age tools

Take children to a woodland area or a suitable space in the school grounds. They will be using natural resources to make Stone Age paint. Ask children to find two stones (you may need to locate these beforehand depending on your location) and give them charcoal. Ask children to grind the charcoal to a fine powder using the two stones. Talk to children about the most effective technique in which to do this – how are they using their stones? Next provide each child with a jam jar (or similar) with some oil in it and ask them to mix their charcoal and oil to create Stone Age paint. When they have mixed their materials they can use the paint to create Stone Age paintings on trees, the ground or rocks around them. Remind them of the types of things Stone Age people would have painted and take a picture as the paintings will wash away.

Back in the classroom

This activity will need to be followed up with classroom discussion. Talk to the children about the difficulties they encountered, for example: managing the stones effectively; finding smooth surfaces on which to grind their charcoal; making the paint smooth enough to be workable; using natural resources as paint brushes which may have given less than the desired effects. Children should then have more of an understanding of the struggles of life in the Stone Age and an appreciation of how people used to live.

2. Making and using Stone Age tools

From doing the activity above children already know that life in Stone Age times was difficult as resources were limited but the Stone Age people were very skilled in making tools and weapons for survival. Set children a challenge: look at pictures of tools and weapons and discuss how they would have been made.

- How were they fixed together?
- How were tools and weapons sharpened and moulded?
- How easy would this have been to do?

Take children outside and ask them to make a weapon or tool from the resources in the natural environment. It is important to point out that the natural environment has changed in the last few thousand years but this should help them to understand the level of skill involved. This is not replication but an interpretation of Stone Age tools.

Back in the classroom
Ask the children to tell you about their tool or weapon.

- What is it?
- What would it have been used for?
- How difficult or easy was it to make?
- How would they develop it further?

This activity will give the children an understanding of the skill of the Stone Age people but also of the constraints placed on them by the lack of resources compared to those we have at our disposal today. They should also gain some sense of the time it would have taken to make an effective tool or weapon and therefore consider the value placed on these items.

Points to note
When learning about the Stone Age it is important for children to develop an understanding of how people lived in the past and the reasons why they led the lives they did. They can make comparisons with our lives today but ensure that they realise how sophisticated the Stone Age period was and its significance in history. It is also important to point out that the Stone Age spanned a long period and that there was clear progression across this period.

WHAT WAS IT LIKE IN THE BRONZE AGE?

A little bit of knowledge...

The Bronze Age is generally thought to have begun around 2000BCE. This is the period that links the Stone Age and the Iron Age and is significant because it is believed that during this period of time there was movement from mainland Europe to Britain and the people who came to Britain brought new ideas, tools and weapons along with a different way of life.

In the Bronze Age the people farmed and worked the land and developed more sophisticated tools and textiles. They also developed pottery and implements that are similar to those used today such as beakers, and other pots used for food preparation and decoration.

Archaeologists have discovered distinctive bell-shaped drinking vessels which were thought to have been brought to Britain by the Beaker people who integrated with the native population and gave rise to what is known as the Wessex culture. There have been pre-historic items discovered from this period that are very detailed and elaborate; including gold and amber elements. Some of these items were so like the Mycenaean culture from Greece that historians believe that this is proof that there was trade between Britain and Greece at the time; providing further evidence that trade and migration was prevalent during the Bronze Age.

How did the Bronze Age civilisations compare in Britain and Greece?

There is evidence that the Bronze Age civilisations of Britain and Greece traded and travelled as many Mycenaean artefacts have been found outside of Greece in places such as Germany, Georgia and Ireland as well as Wessex and Cornwall in England.

Activity

Comparing two cultures

Children should use their skills of deduction and inference to ask questions about how bronze was used in the past in both Greece and Britain. Use questions to structure children's investigations.

Show children images of a Beaker pot from Britain and a Mycenean pot from Greece

Key questions:
How important was bronze to people living at this time?
How do you know?
Look at the pots – what are the similarities and differences?
How would these pots have been used?
How can we use these images to help us learn about what life was like at this time?
What questions do you have that need to be explored?
How will you find your information?
What sources will you use?

How does archaeological evidence help us learn about the past?

Archaeology is the study of the past through observation and analysis of things that have been left behind. Archaeologists use artefacts to help them build up a picture and reconstruct the past, using evidence to ask and answer questions. However, evidence is subject to interpretation and therefore there may be more than one explanation. The more evidence we have, the easier it is to build a true representation of the past.

Activities

1. *Archaeological discovery*

Explain to children the role of an archaeologist. Make links to materials and their properties in the science curriculum and ask children to think about why some things have survived for archaeologists to investigate and others have not. Children are to imagine that they have been buried in the clothes that they are wearing; what would be left in 1000 years' time for archaeologists to use as a source of evidence to find out about their lives? What questions would the archaeologist not be able to answer?

Artefact	Archaeological evidence	Questions the archaeologist might ask
Skeleton bones	Yes	How old was this person? Were they male or female? Did they have any injuries?
Gold earrings	Yes	Why did they wear these? What were they made from? Were they worn by all people or only some members of society?
Clothing	Not likely to survive (depends on material and conditions of burial)	What clothes did they wear? What were their clothes made of? What was the clothing for? Warmth? Ceremonial dress? What other evidence do we need to look for?
Money	Yes	

2. *Who is the Amesbury Archer?*
The Amesbury archer was found in 2002 in Amesbury in Wiltshire during the building of a new school. It is the law that all sites must be surveyed by an archaeologist before building work can take place and any remains or artefacts must be excavated first. The archaeologists were expecting to find artefacts from Roman times but instead discovered some Beaker pots from 2500 years before the Romans. This caused much excitement but significantly delayed the building of the new school. Show children an image of

the gold hair tresses found at the excavation site and ask children to form some enquiry questions such as:

- What are they?
- What were they used for?
- Who would have used them?
- How do we know?
- How can we find out?

Children should use this as a starting point for investigating a wider enquiry question: Who was the Amesbury Archer?

A suggested structure could be:

1. initial stimulus
2. ask questions to generate an enquiry
3. research and collect evidence
4. analyse evidence
5. draw conclusions
6. ask further questions.

What questions can we ask about the Bronze Age?

In the Bronze Age period the tools and weapons became far more sophisticated as metals were introduced; copper and gold to begin with and later bronze which is a combination of copper and tin. There is far more archaeological evidence from the Bronze Age than from the Stone Age as there were a number of new tools and artefacts developed. Some of these new artefacts included small ornaments made of gold, copper knives and a new style of pottery (introduced by the Beaker people) including detailed arrow heads. Many of the items made from copper were probably used for decorative purposes rather than as weapons as copper is too soft to make it an appropriate metal for weaponry.

Activities

1. *Bronze Age true or false?*

Provide children with cards with names of artefacts from the Bronze Age along with definitions of their true meaning. The children's challenge is to offer the class two different definitions for the artefact – one that is true and one they have made up. The class have to listen to both definitions and decide which one is true and which is false, giving their reasons. This could be played individually or in pairs with one child stating the true definition and the other the false.

Beaker pot	**bone toggle**
T: Pottery that was brought from mainland Europe and was a drinking vessel. F:	T: Toggle carved from animal bone and used for fastening clothes. F:
gold bangle	**hanging pots**
T: Gold objects found in graves of important and high status people. F:	T: Pots that had holes around the rim that could have been used to attach cord and hang up. Their exact use is unknown. F:
antler pick	**thumb pot**
T: A tool used for digging pits and ditches (similar to a pick-axe). F:	T: A little pot made by hand. F:
shovel	**flint knife**
T: Made from a cow's shoulder blade; used for digging ditches. F:	T: A sharp knife with very detailed workmanship. F:
bone pin	**gold ornament**
T: Pins made from animals and used for fastening clothes. F:	T: Made from gold and could have been worn wrapped around a lock of hair. F:

2. *Asking questions about the Bronze Age*
Provide children with questions to investigate about the Bronze Age using a grid to structure their thinking. They could add any supplementary questions that they wish to investigate.

What do I already know about the Bronze Age?	What would I like to know about the Bronze Age?	What have I found out about the Bronze Age?

Discuss the importance of validating evidence and looking for more than one source of evidence to corroborate findings.

Examples of questions could be:

Why did the later Bronze Age people begin to cremate their dead instead of bury them?
Why did Bronze Age men wear short skirts and the women wear long skirts?

3. *Surviving the Bronze Age*
Ask children to think about the things they would need to survive daily life in the Bronze Age. Get them to make a list of essentials (e.g. sharp tool for cutting, shelter) and then rank them in order of priority. They could also discuss desirable items and begin to think about how these items would have enhanced their lives.

Are the Beaker people significant to the Bronze Age?

The Beaker people or bell-beaker people got their name from the distinctive pottery that they designed which was bell-shaped. They are believed to have arrived in Britain via the South West coast as it was rich in copper and tin. These people were not invaders but mixed happily with the communities that they settled in. Archaeologists have discovered beakers in many tombs and henges throughout Britain and it is thought that this is evidence that they mixed with the indigenous population on good terms. They improved the existing henge or temple at Stonehenge and created the Avebury monument.

Activities

1. ***Beaker people***

Using a source sheet look at a picture of a Bronze Age beaker and begin to ask questions about the beaker as a source of evidence.

Insert an image of a Bronze Age beaker (available free from historical websites)		
What can I **observe?**	What do I **wonder?**	What do I **infer?**

2. ***Making Bronze Age beakers***

For this activity you will need clay or modelling materials; water and natural materials such as sticks, twigs and leaves for shaping and decorating.

Ask children to roll out their clay into a cylindrical shape and mould it into a beaker shape in a concentric manner. Use fingers and water to smooth the sides before decorating with the natural materials collected. Children can look at pictures of pots to see the patterns used – lines, zig zags and circles were common.

WHAT WAS IT LIKE IN THE IRON AGE?

A little bit of knowledge . . .

The Iron Age takes us from approximately 800BCE until the Roman invasion in 43CE and saw the introduction of iron work although it did not become commonly used until much later. Iron Age people began to form groups and communities and this was a time of migration to Britain which led to rapid economic, social and population growth. Farming became more sophisticated and this led to a wider variety of crops which included barley, wheat, peas and beans. There was an increase in leisure activities such as weaving, practising sling shot and brewing and drinking beer whilst socialising with other members of the community. People in the Iron Age also began to take more of an interest in their appearance and began to dye clothes for aesthetic purposes and accessories began to form a decorative as well as a functional purpose.

The Iron Age people usually lived in roundhouses. A round house was made of timber with walls made from wattle and daub and thatched roofs. The main feature was the fire which was in the centre and provided a source of food, warmth and light. The fire also provided a way to smoke and dry fish and meats as well as drying plants and herbs. This, along with the more sophisticated farming, led to a varied diet.

What was life like for the Iron Age Celts?

Homes and families

The Celts usually lived in wattle and daub roundhouses. Throughout the Celtic period many Iron Age hill forts were established; they varied in size: some would only house one family and others were larger to house the extended family. The fire was a focal point being in the centre of the house with a hole in the roof to allow the smoke to escape; this provided a source of heat and was also used for cooking. The Celts lived in an extended family unit and may have shared responsibility for raising each others' children.

Activities

1. *Making a hill fort*

Ask children to design their own hill fort based on the following criteria.

A hill fort must:

- have a palisade fence to keep out enemies
- be on top of a steep slope
- have trenches dug around it to make it difficult for enemies to get in
- have an enclosed gate that makes it harder for enemies to enter
- keep farm animals to provide, milk, eggs and food
- include somewhere to house the animals
- have a communal area for gathering.

Children can make a virtual hill fort on the computer; draw or paint their hill fort; create a bird's eye view image, make a map, make a model or simply describe their hill fort design. The key here is that they understand the purpose of the design and reasons why Celts chose to live in hill forts.

2. *Odd one out*

Give children a grid with four items that may have been used by Iron Age Celts. One of them is not correct. Children should identify the one that is the odd one out and explain why.

severed head	loom
fire dogs	fire cats

cauldron	stone circles
kettle	shield

animals	gate
palisade fence	barbed wire

chimney	hole in roof
animal skins	spoons

torc	earrings
brooch	watch

milk	berries
meat	bananas

What can we learn about the Iron Age from the evidence the Celts left behind?

As we move further through time there is more evidence available for archaeologists to study and the Iron Age Celts have left behind lots of clues to help us ask and answer questions about their lives. The Celts were not one homogenous group; they shared similar cultures and languages but lived in tribal communities – they were not governed by one state or way of life. They originated from all over Europe but eventually migrated and settled in Britain. The Iron Age Celts worked the land and rose with the sun to work on the farm and tend to the animals. The children would have played, although there is little evidence of this, but they were also expected to help out on the farm.

Both Celtic men and women wore jewellery. It was made from gold, bronze or iron and many of the pieces were highly decorative and would have been worn by nobility, land owners or warriors. Some jewellery was used as a functional part of clothing but other pieces were purely decorative.

Activities

1. Iron Age (Celtic) jewellery

Look at designs and images of Celtic jewellery and ask children to design their own pieces of jewellery for a specific purpose: decoration; a clothing accessory or as a symbol of status or honour.

This could be extended into an art, craft and design activity and children could make their jewellery out of salt dough; mod rock, clay or wire.

After making their jewellery they could explain:

- Who their item is for.
- What is its purpose?
- Why they chose to design it such a way.
- What does it represent?

2. *The Celtic knot*

An alternative craft activity to the one above could involve researching Celtic knots. Celtic knots are used as a representation of the interconnection of life and eternity and are complete loops with no beginning or end. It is believed that Celtic knots were linked to myths and ancient traditions. Ask children to research the stories behind Celtic knots and design their own Celtic knot from chosen material – clay and wood work well. Children should then write a paragraph about the meaning or 'story' behind their Celtic knot based on their research.

What can we learn from written accounts?

The Iron Age Celts had no written language, however, there were written accounts of their lives by the Roman invaders towards the end of the Iron Age period which help us to find out about what life was like in the Iron Age.

Activity

Using written accounts as a source of evidence

Using written evidence from some Roman sources such as Julius Caesar or Diodorus Siculus, ask children to ask questions and make assertions using their skills of inference and deduction.

Below are examples of written accounts by Diodorus Siculus:

> [The Celts] wear bronze helmets with figures picked out on them, even horns, which made them look even taller than they already are... while others cover themselves with breast-armour made out of chains. But most content themselves with the weapons nature gave them: they go naked into battle... Weird, discordant horns were sounded, [they shouted in chorus with their] deep and harsh voices, they beat their swords rhythmically against their shields.

> In exactly the same way as hunters do with their skulls of the animals they have slain... they preserved the heads of their most high-ranking victims in cedar oil, keeping them carefully in wooden boxes.

Below are examples of written accounts by Julius Caesar:

> The common folk are less than nothing and 'treated almost as slaves'.

> The Druids are 'concerned with divine worship, due performance of sacrifices, public and private, and the interpretation of ritual questions: a great number of young men gather about them for the sake of instruction and hold them in great honor'.

Show children the sources and begin to ask questions such as:

- Who wrote this?
- When was it written?
- Why was it written?
- How trustworthy is this source?

Children could place statements in order of validity: Which recount is the most valid and why?

Concluding activities

1. *Comparing ages*

Following a study on the Stone Age, Bronze Age and Iron Age it is useful to ask children to make comparisons between the periods they have studied and to begin to justify their opinion using the knowledge and understanding they have gathered during their studies. Pose a question for the children to answer individually, in pairs or in groups: When do you think it was better to live – Stone Age, Bronze Age or Iron Age? Why? This could lead to discussion and debate.

2. *Timeline connections*

Make a large timeline of the Stone Age, Bronze Age and Iron Age and then extend this by adding key dates from events that were happening outside of Britain at these times. Ensure that the timeline reflects the distance between the periods of time and the length that this happened; this can be done representatively. This timeline can be added to when you move on to studying different periods of history. This will help the children to see connections within and across periods of time and give them an understanding of chronology.

CHAPTER 2
The Egyptians and Ancient Greeks

The activities in this chapter provide ways in which children can begin to understand what life was like thousands of years ago and the legacy that ancient civilisations have left for people living today. These civilisations spanned many, many years and therefore it is not possible to study the whole period in depth; however, the activities in this chapter will give children the interest and opportunities to investigate further.

When people think of Egypt they usually picture the pyramids. These were mainly built as tombs and were a feat of engineering: taking years to build and involving thousands of men. The pyramid of Khufu at Giza is the largest Egyptian pyramid. The afterlife was incredibly important and Egyptians were buried with their worldly possessions in order to carry them to the afterlife with them. Life in Ancient Egypt was centred on the Nile River; the Egyptians were able to manage the flooding and controlled irrigation which led to an abundance of fertile crops.

Another ancient civilisation was the Ancient Greeks who lived nearly 4000 years ago in Greece and other countries that are now called Turkey and Bulgaria. The Ancient Greek Empire was vast and stretched as far as France; they were at the pinnacle of their power from 2000BCE to 146BCE. There were many different Greek states which had their own laws, money and government. Two of the most important states at that time were Athens and Sparta.

WHO WERE THE EGYPTIANS?

A little bit of knowledge . . .

Egyptian society was class led and status was very important. Farmers made up the bulk of the population but artists and craftsmen were considered of a higher status. The upper class displayed their social status in art and literature. Ancient Egyptians viewed men and women from all social classes as equal under the law, however, this was open to interpretation but we do know that Cleopatra and Queen Hatshepsut had positions of high power in Ancient Egypt. The Ancient Egyptians engaged in trade and exported grain, gold, linen and goods such as glass and stone objects. Egyptians believed in the afterlife and were buried with their worldly goods so that they may have them in the afterlife. They made offerings and prayers to gods. They were also embalmed which is a process that preserves the body as they believed they re-entered their body in the spirit world. This began by pulling their brains out through their nose and then removing organs and placing them in four jars so that they did not decompose. The body was then covered with salt for forty days until it mummified. They gave the body artificial eyes and then wrapped the body in bandages, leaving a small gap for the mouth. It was then placed in a body shaped tomb called a sarcophagus: these were decorated elaborately and then placed in a pyramid or tomb and then the tomb was filled with the person's worldly goods in readiness for the afterlife.

How were the pyramids built?

There has been much debate about how pyramids were built though it is widely acknowledged that they were a huge feat of engineering for the time and resources the Egyptians had at their disposal. Techniques developed over time and most historians believe that huge stones were carved with copper chisels and then dragged and lifted into position using ropes and pulleys, and later, sets of ramps. It is thought that the pyramids were formed using stairs so that tiers could be made higher and higher; this would have been a very risky business (there was no safety equipment) and would have involved thousands of men.

Activities

1. Pyramid builders

For this activity you will need:

- four skipping ropes
- an upside down table.

You will also need to divide the children into groups of five or six. One group will stand on the upturned table and the other group will use the skipping ropes (tied to the table legs) to try and pull the children and the table along the floor. This should prove difficult and will give children the opportunity to realise the importance of team work, strength and technique when moving large, heavy objects with limited equipment.

2. Egyptian artefacts

Research the building and significance of pyramids in Egyptian times and discuss the advanced techniques used as well as the commitment needed.

Pupils can then be challenged to make their own pyramid. They could start by doing this on a small scale and using blocks to recognise the difficulties of aligning blocks into a specific pyramid shape before moving on to a larger scale model (perhaps in the playground) where they use foam blocks and work as a team to build a pyramid that is taller than them. This should generate a discussion about the difficulties of building a pyramid and make comparisons to how structures are made today: the Egyptians were able to build structures to a great height without the use of a crane.

What did the Ancient Egyptians believe about death?

The Egyptians strongly believed in the afterlife. Poor Egyptians were buried in the sand while rich Egyptians were buried in a tomb and their bodies preserved using the process of mummification. Some wealthy Egyptians spent many years planning their death at great cost; building tombs and decorating them elaborately. Two of the most well known tombs of Ancient Egypt are that of Tutankhamen and Queen Hatshepsut and the great pyramid of Khufu in Giza (one of the seven wonders of the Ancient World).

Activities

1. *Burial customs*

Investigate the customs surrounding burial and look at the reasons why people were buried with certain items. Egyptians believed in the afterlife and wanted to take their possessions with them as they believed that they could take their wealth to the afterlife. Egyptians were buried with items such as: clothing, shoes, jewellery, perfumes, musical instruments, games, tableware, food (preserved meats and grains), wine and beer as well as furniture. Looking at the items that were commonly found in tombs what does this tell us about the way that Egyptians lived their lives? Ask pupils to think about what their prized possessions are and what they would 'take with them'. Compare the items that are important to us today and those that were of significance to the Ancient Egyptians.

2. *Ethical questions*

Give pupils a question to explore: Is it right to open a sarcophagus? Would this be acceptable in this time and age? Morally, were the explorers correct to have invaded the tombs in the way that they did? Look at the debate surrounding the discovery of the tomb of Tutankhamen which was discovered by archaeologist Howard Carter in 1922. This tomb was not one of the most elaborate but was the most intact – many tombs were robbed long before archaeologists discovered them so finding this was seen as a significant discovery. There were over 3500 items found; most of which are in the Egyptian museum in Cairo. Use the table below to structure the children's responses.

Reasons to open the tomb/sarcophagus	**Reasons not to open the tomb/sarcophagus**
It will help us understand how the Egyptians lived	This is a sacred site where someone has been buried. How would we feel if it was our family member being dug up and their grave disturbed?
We may find treasures and artefacts that are worth lots of money	This is robbery – the possessions are not ours to take

Use the responses from the above activity to structure a discursive writing activity using the following sentence starters:

As I see it…
In my opinion…
Despite the fact that…
In spite of…
Others believe…
Therefore…
In conclusion…

How did the Ancient Egyptians worship?
The Ancient Egyptians worshipped a variety of gods and goddesses. The beliefs and rituals surrounding these gods formed the basis of religion in Ancient Egypt. The gods and goddesses represented natural phenomena and rituals were performed and offerings given as ways of appeasing the gods. Pharaohs were seen to be representative of the gods and managed the offerings and rituals carried out in the temples. The characteristics of the gods were expressed in myths and their appearance was represented in art, as animals and animal and human combinations and symbols.

Activities

1. *Egyptian gods*

Ask children to research the gods and goddesses outlined below. Once they have found out what roles these gods played they can use the information to begin to ask and answer questions about how the Egyptian people lived their lives and what role the gods and goddesses had in their day-to-day lives.

Anubis	Anubis was the god of embalming and the dead
Bastet	
Hapy	
Hathor	
Nephthys	
Osiris	
Ra	
Sekhmet	
Seshat	
Thoth	

2. *Egyptian myths and legends*

Before beginning this activity, immerse the children in Egyptian myths and legends and talk about the impact of these 'stories' on the lives of the Egyptian people. Egyptians worshipped the sun, moon and stars but also believed in magic and the underworld. Use the information above to create a myth based on an existing Egyptian legend of gods and goddesses such as the legend of Osiris. Provide children with guidelines for their writing such as:

Name of god or goddess	Name of hero (main character)	The quest (a challenge set by the god)	How the challenge is won	The result

What was daily life like for Ancient Egyptians?

The people of Ancient Egypt highly regarded family life; children were a blessing and in the lower classes mothers were responsible for the day-to-day care of the children and running the home. Wealthy Egyptians such as nobles and royalty had a range of slaves and servants to cater for their every whim and help them to raise their children. Women obeyed their husbands but Egyptian wives and mothers were highly respected in society. Boys were sent to work with their fathers and learnt a trade or skill whereas girls remained at home with their mothers and learnt from them. Some wealthy boys were sent to school to learn to read, write and work with numbers and it may have been the case with some girls too although there is little evidence of this.

Activities

1. Research artefacts

Using reputable sources such as museum websites download a number of images of artefacts from Egyptian times – try to choose a wide variety of images and consider whether you show children images of replicas or original artefacts and whether they are from reliable sources.

Ask children to use the images to help them find out about what daily life may have been like. The grid below can be used to support children in structuring their ideas:

Family life	Housing and homes	Cooking
Clothing and jewellery	Entertainment	Hair and cosmetics

2. *Hieroglyphs*

Hieroglyphics is one of the ancient Egyptian forms of writing; it was used mainly by priests and is still found today on temple walls and artefacts. It was quite time consuming to write and although it looked beautiful on the walls of temples and tombs it was not appropriate for daily use so most Egyptians used a simpler form of script known as hieratic. Ask pupils to look at the hieroglyphic alphabet (freely available online) and write their name before making their own hieroglyphic codes to write a message for their friends to crack. Encourage the children to look closely at the shapes used in the alphabet and their significance, for example animals are a dominant symbol and the direction the animal is facing highlights the direction in which the text should be read.

3. *What do we know?*

Following on from the two activities above ask children to think about what they know for sure (more than one source of evidence suggests this); what they think they know (one source of evidence available) and what they still need to find out.

WHO WERE THE ANCIENT GREEKS?

A little bit of knowledge . . .

Greek history can be traced back to the Stone Age; approximately 2500 years ago the country was broken up into city states each of which had a city and some countryside. This is known as the Classical Period (500–336BCE) and signified the introduction of government and a new kind of conflict over power. The Ancient

Greeks lived in mainland Greece, on Greek islands and in some parts of Turkey, North Africa and France. Their daily life was much admired and copied by other civilisations such as the Romans.

Ancient Greek society has had an impact on the way we live our lives today. They started the Olympic Games and had a democratic state where the people were able to have a say in the way their country was governed. Greek society was made up of citizens (men who were born in the state) and non-citizens (women, slaves and people not from the Greek states). All citizens could vote for new laws in a system known as the assembly. Men and women in Greek society had different roles. For example, in the Agora (the centre of the Greek market place) the men would meet to discuss politics whereas women were not allowed in the agora unaccompanied and would send their slaves to collect their goods and shop for them. Women in Greek society had to do exactly as their husbands or fathers said and it was their job to run the household and manage servants.

Why are some Greek people still remembered today?

Ancient Greek people have made significant contributions to modern society in a variety of different areas such as: literature, art, science, maths and politics as well as giving us the Olympic Games.

Activities

1. Significant Greeks

Look at the list of famous Greeks that follows and ask children to research in groups to find out about their lives and why they are still remembered today. Sources from the time may be limited (primary sources) so the children may have to rely on secondary sources – remind them that they must consider who wrote the piece; when it was written and for what purpose. They can then relay their information to the rest of the class as a presentation or via a carousel where they move round in groups and learn about each significant person.

Significant people to research (suggestions):

Females	Helen of Troy, Penelope of Ithaca
Philosophers	Socrates, Plato, Aristotle
Playwrights	Sophocles, Aristophanes
Poets	Aesop, Homer
Scientists	Archimedes, Pythagoras, Hippocrates
Leaders	Alexander the Great, Draco
Historians	Herodotus, Thucydides

2. *Justify your opinions*

Ask pupils to look at the above list of famous people from Ancient Greece and to think about who they feel is the most significant and why, justifying opinions and thinking about which person has had an impact on their lives today. Use the following criteria to support the pupils' discussions and decisions:

- How significant was the person at the time?
- Would they be significant today?
- What does their legacy tell us about the lives of people in Ancient Greece?
- What is their impact on today's society?

What are the Olympic Games and how have they changed?

The Olympic Games were recorded as beginning around 776BCE in Olympia. It was a series of athletic competitions, held every four years, and each city state of Ancient Greece was allowed to send representatives. There was a truce held for the duration of the games so that warring states could compete alongside each other. It was held in honour of the god Zeus and a huge statue of him was erected in Olympia, which was one of the seven wonders of the Ancient world. The games consisted not only of athletic competitions but religious celebrations and artistic events; the games were also used as a political platform where leaders from city states could use their athletes and artists to hold political dominance and also to create alliances with other states. Prizes were usually wreaths or crowns made of olive leaves and branches.

Activities

1. The Olympic Games

Ask pupils to compare and contrast the Ancient Greek Olympic Games and the Modern Olympic Games in order to understand the reasons for the changes, for example changing society and development in sports as well as the role of women in society and globalisation of sport.

	Ancient Olympic Games	Modern Olympic Games
Competitors		
Location		
Events		
Length		
Awards		
Organisation		
Frequency		

Look at the medal winners from previous modern Olympic Games and begin to ask questions about equity and social justice such as: Where do most of the winners in certain events come from? How many competitors do certain countries enter in events? Which sports are more popular with spectators? (This could be compared to the Ancient Greek games where the chariot racing was most popular as it was the most dangerous). Which country has won the most gold medals in the last five Olympic Games? Why is this?

2. Looking at artefacts

In this activity children will need to use their visual literacy skills (understand, interpret and evaluate images) and study an image of an Ancient Greek artefact before using it to ask and answer historical questions. Look at images from historical websites such as www.heritage-explorer.co.uk of Olympic Events recorded on pottery. Ask children to think about what this tells them about the Olympic Games – what events were held, what skills would the athletes need, which event do they think would be the most popular, what does that tell us about what life was like at that time? Look at the equipment and clothing – how is this different to the equipment and outfits in today's games? Below are some examples of the original Olympic Games events.

wrestling	javelin	pentathlon
running	boxing and wrestling (pankration)	horseracing
chariot racing	running in armour	long jump

3. *Training and competing*

Competing in the Olympic Games was seen as a huge honour and winners were treated like modern-day sporting stars in their home villages; being adorned with gifts and one even having a personal gym built in his home state. Look at the historical accounts below of the expectations of training for the Olympic Games – what do these accounts tell you about how important this was in Greece?

> If you have worked in a manner worthy of coming to Olympia, and have done nothing in an offhand or base way, proceed with good courage; but as for those who have not so exercised, go away wherever you like.
>
> (Source: unknown)

> not to be prepared beforehand is stupidity, for the minds of the unpractised [sic] are insubstantial things.
>
> (Greek poet: Pindar)

> You must live by rule, submit to diet, abstain from dainty meats, exercise your body perforce at stated hours, in heat or in cold; drink no cold water, nor, it may be, wine. In a word, you must surrender yourself wholly to your trainer, as though to a physician.
>
> (Philosopher: Epictetus)

What was life like in Ancient Greece?

Life for men and women in Ancient Greece was very different; Greek women had to obey their fathers and then their husbands and had very few rights. Their lives were centred on the home and many women were rarely allowed out; spending most of their time with immediate family and their servants. Sparta women had slightly more freedom in their city state; they were taught to read and write and had knowledge of art and literature and were physically fit and healthy. Men were expected to take an active role in the city state and spent much of their time training and discussing politics.

The Ancient Greeks were known for their pottery and it was often used as a way to display their art. They also enjoyed pastimes such as outdoor theatre where they would watch plays: tragedies and comedies which centred on current affairs.

Activities

1. *Greek plays or poems*

Look at an extract from a Greek play (these are available online – they can be quite complex but may be suitable for upper KS2 and KS3 classes) or a poem (provided below)

Water and wine
(Ed 75)

I

Boy! Bring water and bring wine
and bring garlands of flowers

that I may do a round or two with Eros

II

Boy! bring here a cup!
and
Boy! mix ten cups of water to five of wine
and

Boy! let me not shut my lips but let me drink
and drink and rage like
a frenzied Bacchus with
impunity.

III

Come, friends! let's not shout and scream
like Scythian drunks
but
let us study our wine, friends
and
accompany its drinking with beautiful songs

Prayer to Dionysius
(Ed 2)

Please, Dionysius!
Leader of all, whose friends are the omnipotent
Eros and the blue-eyed
Nymphs and the rosy
Aphrodite
and whose compass

is the high peaks of mountains.

Please, be kind enough to come to me and
hear my plea with a smile:

Go, God, and counsel Cleovoulos well and make him
accept my love!

Ask pupils to look for clues – what can they learn about Greek society by looking at the play or poems? Alternatively, this could also be done by looking at artwork and sculptures such as: vessels, images of the Parthenon, statues and commemorative plates.

2. *Philosophy for children*

Using a genuine Plato quote, ask the children to discuss the quote. What does this quote tell us about Greek society? There are many quotes available online such as:

> Good people do not need laws to tell them to act responsibly, while bad people will find a way around the laws.
>
> You can discover more about a person in an hour of play than a year of conversation.
>
> Opinion is the medium between knowledge and ignorance.
>
> The greatest wealth is to live content with little.

What caused the expansion of the Greek Empire?

War was a part of everyday life in Ancient Greece. City states were fighting with each other all the time and battles were bloody and frequent. Large scale battles across the Greek Empire were also common as the empire battled for power and land. Alexander the Great is possibly the most famous wartime leader and conquered a vast area of land, almost engulfing the Persian Empire with territories such as Egypt, The Indian Punjab, Turkey and Iraq. By the end of his rule the Greek Empire spanned three continents and numerous countries and cities.

Activities

1. *Mapping the Empire*

Ask children to map the Empire: using a map showing the Greek Empire and surrounding countries; ask children to highlight countries that were ruled by the Greek Empire before the rule of Alexander the Great and map his route through the Persian Empire and beyond. Find out what these countries were called in Ancient Greek times and what they are known as today.

2. *Was Alexander the Great a good leader?*

Children can start by looking at their maps from the previous activity to begin to explore this key question. The children should think about what other sources they would need (personal accounts, artwork and artefacts) in order to find out whether Alexander the Great was a good leader or not.

3. The end of the Greek Empire

Use the following questions to begin to hypothesise as to why the Greek Empire fell. Ask children to make a decision based on prior knowledge and inference before researching the real causes of the decline of the Greek Empire.

- What impact did the death of Alexander the Great have on the Greek Empire?
- How could the Ancient Greeks protect their vast empire?
- How did the conflicts between the city states affect the Greek Empire as a whole?
- How do you think a rebel army would try to conquer the Greek Empire?

Ask children to think about whether this could have been prevented and what was the main cause of the decline?

Comparing ancient civilisations

Pupils have learnt about the ancient civilisations of Greece and Egypt. Now ask them to compare them. This can be done in categories as outlined below:

	Ancient Egypt	**Ancient Greece**
Architecture		
Role of women		
Food		
Entertainment		
Education		
Power and politics		
Slaves		
Houses and homes		

Don't forget to update your class timeline to reflect the new periods in history that you have learnt about.

CHAPTER 3
The Romans

WHO WERE THE ROMANS?

A little bit of knowledge . . .

The name Romans comes from the capital city of Italy, Rome, which was at the heart of the Roman Empire. The people of Rome were farmers and herders. Rome quickly became a rich city ruled by kings who had slaves and servants to look after their every need. Rome was governed by a Roman Emperor. The Romans were keen to spread their power and land ownership across Europe and beyond and first came to Britain in 55BCE. In Britain at this time the Celts ruled and there were many different chiefs all fighting for power.

Roman society was divided into two very distinctive groups: the Patricians, who were descended from noble and wealthy families; they owned land and took seats in government. The Patricians only associated with people from their own class. At the other end of the scale there were Plebeians; those people generally worked for the Patricians and had no rights or say over any of the laws.

The Roman Empire spanned many years and did not end quickly. The Empire gradually began to crumble due to the high taxes and fractured society – the rich were very rich but the poor just got poorer. Unfortunately, the money problems led to there not being enough money to pay for essentials like an army to defend them. The Roman Empire spanned such vast distances that huge numbers of soldiers were required to defend their conquests. Barbarians fought against Roman rule and, unfortunately for the Romans, their superb roads and infrastructure made them more vulnerable to attack.

Who was Julius Caesar?

Julius Caesar was born in 100BCE and is one of the most significant Roman figures in history. He came from a wealthy family and was well educated; excelling at sport. Caesar served in the Roman army and became interested in politics; aspiring to climb the political ladder. He began by taking on the role of public entertainment officer – he spent lots of money on high quality entertainment for the people of Rome and this made him very popular with the poor people of Rome. He was sent to Gaul (France) and served as a governor and as general of a large army he conquered more land for Rome. However, although the poor of Rome loved him and his army served him well the people in power in Rome were suspicious of his motives and felt he was too ambitious. They were right to be worried. Caesar led his army to Rome and civil war broke out, with Julius Caesar emerging triumphant as the new dictator of Rome. He began to implement some government reforms and changed the calendar, but became increasingly unpopular in the senate; this eventually led to his murder by a group of conspirators.

Activities

1. The significance of Julius Caesar

Tell children about the life of Julius Caesar; looking at his achievements and the impact they had on different groups in Roman society as well as looking at his downfall. Give children the triangle below, double sided; on one side ask children to think of reasons why Julius Caesar was a good leader and on the other side reasons why he was not a good leader and rank them in order of significance: most important at the bottom and least important at the top.

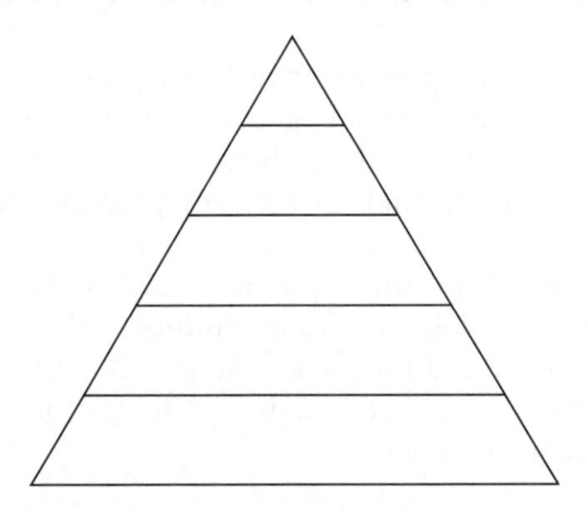

Once the children have written their thoughts and ordered them in terms of significance they can then use this information to create a piece of writing demonstrating a balanced viewpoint. You can use the sentence starters below to structure the children's writing.

> *Julius Caesar is a significant figure in Roman history because________.*
>
> *He was a good leader because he ________________, however, he also________________ which meant that ____________________________________.*
>
> *Some people did not want Julius Caesar to become leader of Rome because ________________.*
>
> *I think that ______________________.*

2. *Representations of Caesar in history*

Because Julius Caesar was a significant figure there are many representations of him and his character, but not all of these are from viable sources. Look at the following four written sources of evidence and consider how Julius Caesar has been represented. The children can build up a picture of Caesar from each source, and consider: if I had only this source to rely on I would think Caesar was... The children can also look for common threads across all four sources and begin to consider what this means – is it true as it has been cited in four different sources? When looking at written evidence remember to always ask the children to consider the following: Who wrote it? When was it written? What was the purpose? How long after the event was it written? How reliable is this as a source of evidence?

Source 1 by Cicero (member of Roman senate)

Our tyrant deserved to die. Here was a man who wanted to be king of the Roman people and master of the whole world. Those who agree with an ambition like this must also accept the destruction of existing laws and freedoms. It is not right or fair to want to be king in a state that used to be free and ought to be free today.

Source 2 by Brutus (one of Caesar's killers) taken from Shakespeare's play: *Julius Caesar*

Not that I loved Caesar less but I loved Rome more…

Source 3 by Plutarch written 75ACE

When some who were present had begun to raise a cry against Caesar, the people answered with loud shouts and clapping in his favour…and by this show of affection he won upon the feelings of the people, who looked upon him as a man of great tenderness and kindness of heart.

Source 4 by Nicolaus of Damascus (not present at the murder but spoke to those who were)

The conspirators never met openly, but they assembled a few at a time in each others' homes. There were many discussions and proposals,…But the majority opinion favoured killing him while he sat in the Senate, where he would be by himself since non-Senators would not be admitted, and where the many conspirators could hide their daggers beneath their togas. This plan won the day.

3. Julius Caesar's invasion of Britain

Give children some facts about the three invasions of Britain and ask them to begin to use their knowledge to make a judgement as to why these events occurred, justifying their opinions using historical evidence and knowledge of Julius Caesar.

Statement	Questions to reflect on	Interpretation and justification
The British had been helping the Gauls (French) fight against the Roman Army. Julius Caesar sent an army to invade Britain in 55BCE. The army fought the British but no territory was conquered. They returned to Gaul.	Why were the British helping France? Why did Caesar send an army? Why did the Roman army leave? Was it a reconnaissance mission or had they underestimated the power of the British army?	
Julius Caesar returned to Britain in 54BCE with a large army (30,000 + soldiers) and chariots. Caesar captured some land but did not continue to conquer the majority of the country. The army and Caesar returned to Rome.	Why did he return? Why did Caesar return with such a large army? Why did he not stay to conquer the rest of the country? Why did he return to Rome?	

Children may need to explore further sources of information to strengthen their argument and justify their opinions. Ask children to look at the information they already know about Caesar – does this new information about the British invasions change or support their opinion of him?

What was the Roman Empire?

The Roman Empire was one of the largest empires in history and had vast territories across Europe, North Africa and Middle East. Julius Caesar was significant as his promotion to dictator of Rome signified the beginning of the Roman Empire where all the land was ruled by one person. The Roman Empire spanned many years and therefore had an impact on the territories it had conquered in terms of language, culture and architecture. Signs of the Roman Empire can be seen around the world today.

Activities

1. *The Roman army*

Ask children to consider why citizens joined the Roman army – organise the statements below in to advantages, disadvantages or both using a Venn diagram.

Soldiers were paid good money.

Auxiliary soldiers were recruited from invaded countries.

Slaves could be soldiers.

You had to stay in the army for 20 years.

You were not allowed to marry.

You were fed and slept in the barracks.

You had to train for two hours a day.

You had to run 26 miles every month as part of your training.

After 20 years you may be granted freedom.

It was seen as an honour to be in the Roman army.

You were well trained and physically fit.

Soldiers had some free time where they could play games and had entertainment to keep them amused.

2. *Daily life in Roman times*

Ask children to find out what life was like for a Roman soldier and a Roman slave. There is a wealth of information on the web but this is also an opportunity for children to gather research from books; making concise notes and re-writing passages in their own words. Pupils can write a diary extract for the day as if they were a Roman soldier and a Roman slave using the information they have gathered.

3. *Daily life in Rome*

Look at the artefacts in the pictures and use these to begin to build up a picture of what daily life was like in Rome. Recreate the pairs below, sourcing images from the internet to match the text. Try www.history.org.uk for suitable images. Ask children to match the picture with the definition.

Gladiators Slaves were trained to fight one another for the entertainment of Roman people using different weapons and fighting techniques, often to the death. They also used to fight wild animals such as lions and bears and were watched by a large crowd in an amphitheatre.	
Roman baths Rome had many public baths where Roman citizens could go and relax. They used to do exercise before going in to heated rooms to sweat (a bit like a sauna) where slaves would scrape off their sweat (strigil) and they would then plunge into a cold bath.	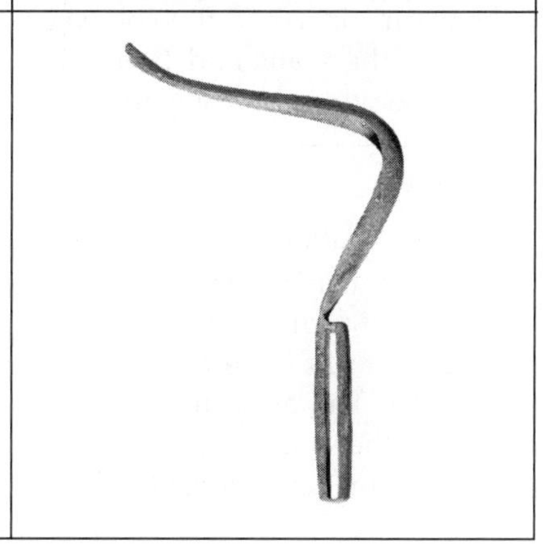

Chariots Chariots were carts that were driven by one man and pulled by four horses. This meant that they went very fast and were raced at great speed for the entertainment of the Roman citizens. They raced around a track seven times and there were many crashes.	
Jewellery Roman jewellery was worn for decoration, good luck or to display wealth. Some jewellery was decorated in the form of snakes, gods and goddesses or gemstones. Some jewellery was also functional, it was used for fastening clothing.	
Heating The Romans had a central heating system called hypocaust. A fire or furnace was kept lit by slaves and the warm air would flow between gaps in the walls and floors and keep the whole house warm.	
Armour Roman soldiers wore their armour when going in to battle but also when marching (other-wise it would have to have been carried!). The armour was made from leather and iron; they wore a metal helmet and carried a shield.	

Weapons The Romans had short swords (for hand to hand combat) and long spears for throwing. The short sword was called a gladius and the long spear was called a pilum.	

Ask children to think about what they think it would have been like to live in Rome. What would they have liked about living in Roman times as a Roman citizen? How would life have been different if they were a Roman slave or a Roman soldier?

4. *Roman legacy*

Show children cards outlining some of the things that the Romans left behind that we can still see today that helps us to remember them (their legacy).

roads	**aqueducts**	**calendar**	**religion**	**roman numerals**
science	**public health**	**laws**	**names**	**Latin**

Divide the children into groups and ask them to research their area finding out more information to share with the rest of the class. Provide a scaffold, for example:

> Religion: What did the Romans believe? What impact has that had on our lives today?
>
> Roman numerals: What are Roman numerals? How and why are they used today?

5. *Importance of Roman legacy*

The Romans had a huge impact on the way we live our lives today, giving us things such as: language, sanitation, irrigation, aqueducts, the calendar, benefits, street cleaners, wine, laws, public libraries, public order, education, public heated baths, cats and stinging nettles. Share out the above innovations between groups and ask each group to formulate an argument as to why their legacy is the most significant. Get children to think about which 'invention' or initiative they could not live without today. Why is it important? How many people's lives has it impacted? What are the knock-on effects of this invention?

Why did the Romans invade Britain in 43CE?

In 43CE under the rule of Emperor Claudius the Romans returned to invade Britain and this time they were successful; conquering parts of Southern Britain which then became part of the Roman Empire. It was not a peaceful invasion however, as Boudicca led a 100,000 strong Celtic army against the Romans' 10,000 men. This attack was not successful and the Romans defeated the Celtic army and pushed through England, conquering more land. However, when they reached Scotland (then known as Caledonia) they met fierce opposition from the Picts and many attempts to invade were thwarted. Eventually Emperor Hadrian built a wall to seal off Caledonia from Britannia (this is known as Hadrian's Wall and parts are still standing today). The Romans settled in Britain for four hundred years and changed the culture of Britain bringing their food, architecture and way of life with them. However, in 383CE the nobles and soldiers left Britain to protect the Roman Empire which was being invaded by barbarians.

Activities

1. *Invasion of Britain*

Divide the class in half and make half the Celts and half the Romans (make hats and helmets to get the children in role) and do an empathy event. The Romans will need to investigate the reasons why they wanted to invade and what they felt they would bring to the country whereas the Celts will need to think of reasons why their way of life needs to be preserved and what they will lose. Children should present their arguments in role; this could then lead on to a writing task where children could write a persuasive piece of text imploring the Romans not to invade or a balanced discussion where they look at both sides of the argument before drawing their own conclusions.

2. *Successful invasion*

The Roman army was successful for a number of reasons:

- organisation
- each soldier had a specific role or duty
- it was a full time job (professional)
- a range of weapons and weaponry
- protective armour
- good at defence as well as attack
- effective leadership
- worked as a team
- well planned attacks
- disciplined soldiers who had been well trained
- commitment to training and keeping fit and healthy.

Show children images from www.history.org.uk of some of the tactical manoeuvres that the Roman army deployed when attacking and invading. Ask children to look at the images, like the ones on the next page, and think about how successful each manoeuvre would have been and how it would have been used.

The manoeuvre	How would this have been used (attack, defence or other?)	How successful and why?
The orb 		
The tortoise 		
The wedge 		
The repel cavalry 		

3. *Boudicca*

In some historical accounts Boudicca is cited as being the Queen of the Icenis who led a revolt against the Roman invasion of Britain. However, the only primary accounts were written by Romans; one of which was written 100 years after her death so it is difficult to know what is true. Split the children into groups and give them different sources of information about Boudicca and ask them to make a profile of her as a person. Who was she? What did she do? What did she look like? Why is she remembered?

Source 1: Statue of Boudicca in Westminster, London

Source 2: Description of Boudicca by Cassius Dio (a Roman historian) written 100 years after her death

In stature she was very tall, in appearance most terrifying, in a glance of her eye most fierce, and her voice was harsh; a great mass of the tawniest hair fell to her hips, around her neck was a large golden necklace and she wore a tunic of many colours.

Source 3: Description of Boudicca from *The Annals* by Tacitus, Book XIV, written 109CE, which tells the story of the rebellion led by Boudicca.

Boudicca, with her daughters before her in a chariot, went up to tribe after tribe, protesting that it was indeed usual for Britons to fight under the leadership of women. 'But now,' she said, 'it is not as a woman descended from noble ancestry, but as one of the people that I am avenging lost freedom…heaven is on the side of a righteous vengeance; a legion which dared to fight has perished; the rest are hiding themselves in their camp, or are thinking anxiously of flight. They will not sustain even the din and the shout of so many thousands, much less our charge and our blows. If you weigh well the strength of the armies, and the causes of the war, you will see that in this battle you must conquer or die. This is a woman's resolve; as for men, they may live and be slaves.'

Source 4: Description of Boudicca from Cassius Dio

…a terrible disaster occurred in Britain. Two cities were sacked, eighty thousand of the Romans and of their allies perished, and the island was lost to Rome. Moreover, all this ruin was brought upon the Romans by a woman, a fact which in itself caused them the greatest shame…But the person who was chiefly instrumental in rousing the natives and persuading them to fight the Romans, the person who was thought worthy to be their leader and who directed the conduct of the entire war, was Buduica, a Briton woman of the royal family and possessed of greater intelligence than often belongs to women…

Source 5: Description of Boudicca from a secondary source

Boudicca led a tribe against Roman rulers and several other tribes joined in with her. They managed to destroy Colchester and it is believed that Boudicca and her people killed 70,000 people in the attacks: Romans and British sympathisers. It is not clear what happened to Boudicca but it is believed that she took poison when she realised that she would not win the battle and feared capture whilst others claim she fell ill and died.

Compare the children's profiles and ask them to discuss how the source of information they used helped them to build up a picture of Boudicca. Why are they so different? This should demonstrate to the children the importance of using more than one source of information and questioning the sources we use for authenticity.

4. Hadrian's Wall

Using the information below about Hadrian's Wall ask children to think about what the evidence tells us about the Romans.

Evidence from Hadrian's Wall	What does this tell us about the Romans?
The wall was built by Emperor Hadrian to separate the Caledonians (Scottish) from the British to protect the Empire.	
Gateways or 'mile castles' were situated at regular intervals along the wall for entrance and exit. These were patrolled.	
The wall was built from stone that was quarried locally. The stonemasons' inscriptions tell us where the stones came from.	
There was a large fort on Hadrian's wall called Vindolanda where some artefacts such as ink on wood documents and letters have been found. These are the oldest surviving handwritten documents in Britain.	
The wall was 73 miles long and was 3 metres wide and approximately 6 metres high.	
A row of forts was built along the wall at regular intervals.	

The Vindolanda tablets are one of the most significant archaeological finds in British history and are thought to be the oldest handwritten artefacts found in Britain. There are a number of translations available online as well as pictures and information that the children could investigate (www.britishmuseum.com).

Living timeline

The Roman period spanned many, many years – often pupils struggle to visualise the time between events and how long this period lasted. This activity should help.

Give half the pupils cards with key roman events and dates on them and the other half key events and dates in history across different time periods (make these on different colours for ease). Arrange the pupils in a human timeline and use distances to show the gap between each event. This activity is best done in the hall or playground.

CHAPTER 4

The Saxons, Vikings and Normans

The activities in this chapter provide ways in which children can begin to understand what life was like following the Roman invasion of Britain. Britain was shaped by the invaders and settlers; each invasion leaving its impact on the lives of the British people. Many of the people in Britain today, who may think they have pure British heritage, are actually a combination of the many civilisations and groups of people who invaded and settled in Britain over the past 2000 years.

At this time the country was divided in to seven kingdoms: Northumbria, Mercia, Wessex, Essex, East Anglia, Sussex and Kent. Consequently, different parts of Britain were ruled by different groups of people. The Anglo-Saxons ruled most of Britain but never managed to conquer Cornwall, Wales and Scotland.

WHO WERE THE ANGLO-SAXONS?

A little bit of knowledge…

The last of the Roman soldiers left Britain in 410CE; this created a gap for new people to come across the North Sea. The new invaders and settlers were not from one location but were made up of groups of people from places such as Northern Germany, Northern Holland and Denmark. These tribes of people were not governed by Roman rule and were referred to as 'barbarians' by the Roman Empire as they would not abide by their laws. The Anglo-Saxons were good sailors and ship builders which enabled them to make the passage to Britain. Most Anglo-Saxons were not

Christians. They had similar beliefs to the Celts in as much as they worshipped gods and goddesses. As a result of Roman occupation most people in Roman Britain were Christians. The Anglo-Saxon name is actually an amalgamation of the three invading tribes called Angle, Saxon and Jute. The Angles and the Saxon tribes were the largest of the attacking tribes and therefore became known as the Anglo-Saxons.

The Anglo-Saxons ruled Britain for about 500 years which is 100 years longer than the Romans. The Anglo-Saxons remained in Britain and many people can trace their ancestry back to Anglo-Saxon times.

Anglo-Saxon towns and villages were ruled by chieftains and the towns often took their names from the ruling chief. Many of these names remain today for example: Hastings takes its name from Haestingas which means Haesta's people.

Who was King Alfred the Great?
King Alfred was King of Wessex for 28 years following the defeat of the Vikings at the Battle of Eddington in May 848CE. This battle created the foundations of the country we now call England and Alfred began to form an organised army and navy and used guerrilla warfare to conquer the invaders. During this time Alfred and his army had to hide in the countryside to plan their attacks; they often had to live alongside ordinary folk and therefore a number of rumours and stories about Alfred and his army have survived. Eventually, the invaders agreed to live alongside the Britons in the county of Wessex with King Alfred as ruler of the county.

How can we use artefacts to find out about Anglo-Saxon times?
'Archaeology' is the study of how people lived in the past. Archaeologists use a variety of evidence to build up a picture of places, people and cultures from the past. The evidence they find is used to support historical interpretation. Artefacts are objects left behind that give us clues to the past.

Obviously, not all artefacts will survive or remain intact so historians rely on a number of sources such as written accounts, images and interpretations as well as artefacts.

Activities

1. *Sutton Hoo*

Make a list of artefacts discovered at the famous Saxon burial site: Sutton Hoo. Place pictures of replicas of the items in the middle of a piece of paper. Ask children to make observations and use the evidence to infer and deduce what life was like during this time. Use the following questions as a guide:

- What was this used for?
- What is it made of?
- Who would have used it?
- Do we still use it today?
- How important was this item to people at the time?
- What do you still need to know in order to answer the questions you may still have?

2. *Interpretations of history*

Following on from the above activity ask children to look at the artefacts they have explored and use these to draw or write what they think the Anglo-Saxon people would have looked like.

Artefacts found (what we know)	What we don't know (need to interpret)
purses	male or female
shoulder clasps	length and colour of hair
gold buckles	skin colour
sword belts (decorated)	colour of clothes
shields	style of clothes
helmet	class or place in society
armour	age

All the drawings or historical accounts are a piece of historical interpretation based on evidence. Make sure that children justify their drawings or accounts using their prior knowledge; explaining what they have drawn or written.

What was the Anglo-Saxon chronicle?

The Anglo-Saxon chronicle is a key piece of historical evidence and is the most important historical source that has survived from this period. It is not an unbiased account but can support interpretations of events and life at the time. It was ordered to be written by King Alfred the Great; many copies were made and they were distributed to monasteries around the country. It was then the job of the monks to keep the chronicle up-to-date when key events occurred. There are nine versions of the chronicle left today but when compared they often give different accounts of the same event and have one-sided views; hence the biased nature of the document.

Activities

1. The Anglo-Saxon chronicle

Use the extracts below from the translated version of the Anglo-Saxon chronicles as a starting point for some text-related activities such as:

1. Sequencing: cut an extract into lines and ask the children to put it back together so that the text makes sense.
2. Prediction: blank out half the words in an extract and see if children can predict what will come next.
3. Transform an extract of the text into something else, for example: a newspaper; a personal letter or diary entry or a storyboard.
4. Using their oral skills ask children to make a radio broadcast or a podcast of the first publication of the Anglo-Saxon chronicles.
5. Children could also each be given a different extract from the text and pick out key vocabulary – find the definition and meaning and create a word board in their groups.

AD 871. And the Danish-men were overcome; and they had two heathen kings, Bagsac and Halfdene, and many earls; and there was King Bagsac slain, and these earls; Sidrac the elder, and also Sidrac the younger, Osbern, Frene, and Harold; and the army was put to flight.

AD 876. And in this same year the army of the Danes in England swore oaths to King Alfred upon the holy ring, which before they would not do to any nation; and they delivered to the king hostages from among the most distinguished men of the army, that they would speedily depart from his kingdom; and that by night they broke.

2. Using written sources

Even though we know that the Anglo Saxon chronicles were a biased text they are still a useful source of evidence in helping us build up a picture of what life was like.

Provide children with an extract and mark up the text as shown below. Use this as a starting point to generate further questions and discussions.

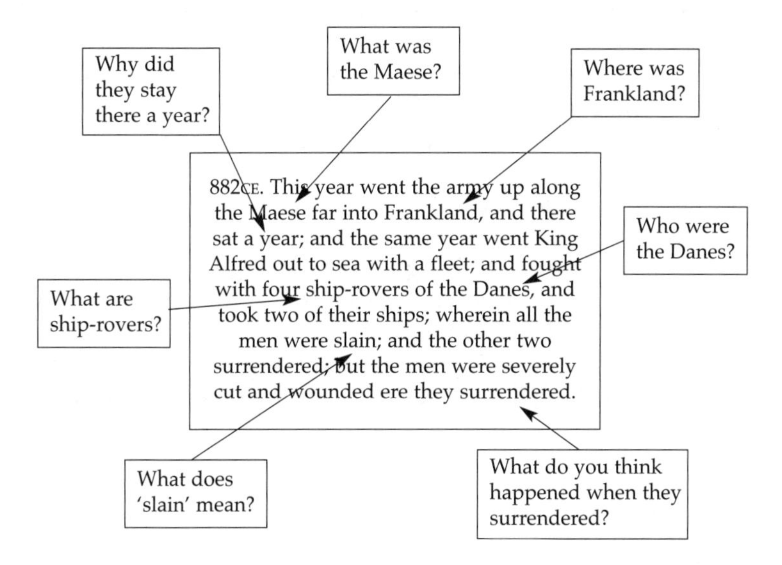

This activity could lead to a number of follow up activities; the children may come up with questions that they can answer easily using their current knowledge but it may also lead to questions they cannot answer which will involve further research.

Activities

1. *The burnt cakes story...*

During Alfred's time in battle with the invaders he engaged in guerrilla warfare which involved spending time hiding out in the countryside and planning attacks. At this time, he was revered amongst his people as Wessex was the only county not to be conquered therefore many people passed down stories about the battles and the attacks. One of these stories is 'The burnt cakes'. Apparently, King Alfred was hiding out in an old lady's cottage when she asked him to watch her cakes that were in the oven. Unfortunately, they burnt and the lady was so cross she began to attack King Alfred; he could have stopped the attack at any time but did not want to reveal his identity. Tell children the story (more detailed versions available online) and ask them to think about the following questions:

- Why do you think that he did not disclose his identity?
- Do you think this story is true? What are your reasons?
- Who would benefit from this story? Who would want it to be passed on?
- Does it match any historical evidence that we have found from reputable sources?
- Does it match your view of Alfred the Great?

2. *King Alfred the Great*

Does King Alfred deserve the title of King Alfred the Great? Ask children to discuss this question. Then give them a bank of statements to arrange on concentric circles. The centre circle will be to place statements of most significance; the next will be 'very significant' followed by 'significant', 'not very significant' and then 'least significant' on the outside of the circle. Statements could include:

King Alfred burnt the cakes	King Alfred ordered the monks to write the Anglo-Saxon chronicles
King Alfred fought the Vikings	King Alfred made peace with the Vikings so they could live in peace
On the coins it stated 'King of the English'	He was advised by a council of nobles and church leaders
He was a good ship builder	He was a good King
Alfred believed that education was important	He was a skilled fighter
He invented many things such as the candle clock	He taught himself Latin and translated many Latin books

Encourage the children to think about who these statements may have been significant to. What if we looked at King Alfred from a different perspective?

WHO WERE THE VIKINGS?

A little bit of knowledge . . .

The Vikings came from three countries: Norway, Sweden and Denmark and there are many interpretations of the meaning of the word Viking, some of which are: 'pirate raid' or 'going on an adventure' (going Viking was used as a verb). The Vikings mainly invaded and settled in the North of Britain (now Scotland) as the southern part of the country had been taken over by the Anglo-Saxons. They first invaded Britain in 793CE and last invaded in 1066 when William the Conqueror became King of England. One of the most famous Viking attacks was the attack on Lindisfarne, the Christian monastery. The Vikings were pagans, not Christians and therefore had no respect for the sanctuary of a Christian place of worship. Commonly regarded as ruthless and vicious fighters once the Vikings had settled they tended to live quite peacefully and were simply searching for better land to farm.

We can tell where Vikings settled by looking at the names of towns and villages in the North of England, Scotland and parts of Wales. Place names ending in –by meant farm or homestead such as Derby, Whitby and Grimsby. Place names ending in –toft meant a place where a house was built such as Lowestoft.

What was a Viking longship?

The Vikings travelled vast distances in their longships and even made it all the way across the Atlantic to America. The ships were seaworthy and were great for raiding as they could be sailed in shallow waters right up to the beach. On the front of the ship there was a fierce creature carved into the wood which was to scare the enemy and it could hold up to 120 people for battle.

Activities

1. *Longships*

How significant was the longship to the Vikings' success?

The Vikings were successful raiders and settlers. Design an enquiry for the children in order for them to answer the question above.

- First, show them a picture of a Viking longship and get them to begin to ask some questions they want to investigate, for example: how many men did it hold? Did women travel on the boat? Why was it built this shape? Did it have a sail? If there was no wind how did it travel?
- Then provide the children with sources of information such as pictures, clips, museum links online; a wide range of books – both fact and fictional; paintings; artefacts and interpretations from the media.
- Using all these sources children should be able to build up a picture of why the ships were central to the success of the Viking raids.
- Encourage children to be critical about the sources they have and ask questions such as: how reliable is this source? When was it produced and for what purpose? Do the sources support or conflict each other?
- What further questions do children have that could not be answered by their enquiry?

2. *On board a Viking longship*

In this activity the teacher will be taking on the role of a Viking warrior on board a longship. Using the information below encourage the children to ask you questions in role to find out about what life was like on board a Viking longship.

Teacher information

- Viking ships were powered by oars and wind.
- The sails were made of wool (although this cannot be proved).
- The oars were different lengths depending on what part of the ship the warriors were seated (due to shape of ship).
- There was no shelter.
- Vikings may have arrived on land at night.
- The sails may have doubled up as shelter.
- Food would have been dried or salted meat or fish (not proven).
- Most voyages were in spring due to weather conditions.
- Vikings did not use maps – they used sun, stars, wind, waves and birds to navigate and possibly, a sundial.
- There were no toilets on the ship.
- They often travelled in large fleets – 350 Viking ships sailed up the Thames in one raid.

Following this activity encourage the children to think about whether the information you gave them was true (how can they corroborate this evidence); what may have been true and what was fabricated.

Children can then write an account of what life was like on Viking longships; when they have finished ask the children to mark up their work using two different coloured pens: underlining information they know to be true in one colour and information they think might be true in another.

What were the Vikings like?

Vikings, as with many groups of people in history, have been stereotyped as ruthless killers, who were only interested in raiding and invading but . . . is this the truth? Many Vikings chose to settle and lived peacefully in established villages alongside the native people.

There were three main classes in Viking society: Jarls (earls and noblemen), Karls (free Vikings) and Thrals (slaves). Once a Viking was a slave he remained a slave for the rest of his life as did his children.

Activity

1. Viking misconceptions

Give children a bank of statements about the Vikings and ask them to sort them in to true or false, justifying their reasons. This activity is best done at the beginning of a project on the Vikings before the children have developed any knowledge.

Ask children to think about what they know about the Vikings and what they still need to find out, for example: I know that there were three classes of Vikings but I do not know what their roles in society were.

True	False
Swansea was named after the Viking King Sweyn.	Vikings had horns on their helmets.
Lots of words we use now have come from Viking times: cake, shy, kitchen, husband, awkward.	A Vikings most treasured possession was his shield.
Lots of words we use now have come from Viking times: anger, berserk, kidnap, ransack, scream.	All Vikings continued to fight even after they had invaded a town or village.
Once Vikings had invaded they settled peacefully in North west Scotland, North east England and parts of Wales.	Two Famous Viking leaders' nicknames were: Victor the Vicious and Harold the Happy.
Some Viking leaders were known by their nicknames such as: Eric Bloodaxe and Harold Bluetooth.	Vikings believed it was shameful if they died in battle.
Vikings passed on stories through poems and rhymes to make them easier to remember.	Viking longships had large cabins underneath for the sailors to sleep in.
The nursery rhyme 'London Bridge is Falling Down' is linked to the Viking invaders.	Vikings ruled all of England.
Thursday is named after the Viking God 'Thor'.	Monday is named after the Viking God 'Marc'.
Vikings had three classes of people: Thrals, Karls and Jarls.	Vikings had three classes of people: Flarks, Jarks and Tarks.

Why were gods important to the Vikings?

In Viking times gods were significant and Viking people gave great power to their gods believing them to have control over many aspects of their lives. Vikings did not follow a religion but they did worship gods and idols and made sacrifices to these gods to bring them luck and protect them in battles and on journeys.

Activity

Viking gods

The Viking culture was strongly influenced by mythology and this had an impact on how they lived their lives: they believed that if they died in battle and were worthy they went to Valhalla which was ruled over by Odin. This was deemed a privilege and therefore meant that dying in battle was admired and honoured.

Odin God of war, poetry and wisdom	**Thor** God of thunder, storms and winds	**Friga** Goddess of married love and the family hearth
Freya Goddess of beauty and the night	**Frey** God of fertility	**Loci** Wizard of lies
Idun Goddess of spring and immortal youth	**Hel** Goddess who ruled over the land of the dead: Niflheim	**Bragi** God of poetry, music and the harp
Dagr God of the daytime	**Delling** God of dawn	**Eir** Goddess of healing
Elli Goddess of old age	**Gmot** God of the moon	**Hlin** Goddess of consolation and protection
Magni God of strength	**Ran** Goddess of the sea	**Weth** Goddess of Anger

Play guess who? Give each child the name of a god and ask children to describe their god's role and significance and the other pupils to guess which god they are. Encourage children to think about how their god impacted on the way the Vikings lived their lives.

What was life like for Viking women?

In Viking times women were treated more fairly than women across the rest of Europe at the time. They were seen as almost equal to men and had choices in most things except who they married; this was decided for them by their families when they were between the ages of 12 and 16 years old. Women were expected to run a household and the Viking wife had responsibilities for managing the home, looking after any animals and preparing food as well as caring for the children. When their husbands were away in battle they were responsible for managing the food supply and running the home so had control over many aspects of the day-to-day lives of their families. Women were also adept at sewing and weaving and working the loom; when they married Viking women were allowed to keep their possessions and did not become the property of their husband. Any children born from the marriage were classed as the property of the mother and could not be taken away by the father even if the couple divorced; which was acceptable in Viking times if the husband had treated his wife unfairly. In order to proclaim a divorce the women needed to gather witnesses and divorce was granted.

Activities

1. Viking women

Ask children to read the account of a Viking woman's day and use this to begin to ask and answer questions about the lives of Viking women at that time.

Ask children to highlight all the key information and rewrite it as a list of statements. Begin to think about which are true and false interpretations and how they can find other evidence to support the statements from the text.

A Day in the Life of Agatha: Wife of Eirik

As soon as the light shone through on to the floor I woke quietly without disturbing Eirik and went outside to tend to the animals, my keys jangling on my belt. As the sun rose fully my children Ingrid and Olsen came out to help me and when the animals had been fed we went inside to prepare breakfast. We made porridge and had dried fruit – Eirik's favourite. Although I wanted Eirik to eat well as he was soon due to go away to battle I was also aware that I needed to manage the food that we had left in stores as there was a long winter ahead. Straight after breakfast I set to work; I sent the children to collect berries and to collect the milk from the cows whilst I set to work at my loom making warm clothes for the coming winter months. Eirik would need clothes to keep him warm on the cold seas and the children and I needed blankets to keep us warm in the cold nights. Whilst I am dreading Eirik going away again as I always worry that he won't return, I am looking forward to the arrival of my sister Thora, from a neighbouring village, who is coming to stay with me whilst the menfolk are away. She has recently divorced her man who treated her terribly, eating all the food and not providing for the family. She was very brave and called witnesses from the village to renounce him at her doorway. She is bringing her two children Alva and Gustav to stay with us too. I am hoping she will settle in our village to be close to me as the children are her property and I can support her in caring for them; she will also be able to help me care for the farm which grows daily due to the hard work of my husband Eirik and myself.

2. *Comparing the lives of women*

Using their knowledge of what life was like in Anglo-Saxon, Norman and Viking times ask children to compare the lives of women in the three different societies.

Using the table on the next page ask children to carry out research to find out how lives were different or similar for women in these different time periods.

	Jobs/roles	Status	Marriage	Clothing	Law
Anglo-Saxon women	Cheese-makers Dairy maids Bakers Spinners Weavers				
Viking women			Could divorce their husbands		
Norman women					Could not own land unless they were widowed

Use the information gathered to compare and contrast the lives of women. Begin to ask and answer questions such as:

- Which women had most freedom?
- Why do you think the role of women changed?
- How do Anglo-Saxon, Viking and Norman women's roles compare with women's roles today?

What was Valhalla?

Vikings believed that if they died in battle they would enter Valhalla, which was a heavenly place where they could drink, fight and enjoy many delights. If Vikings did not die in battle they were put in Viking hell where the walls were lined with snakes' spines and they had to drink goat's urine! This could be a reason why the Vikings were such fierce fighters; they were not afraid to die in battle and dying in this way was seen to be honourable and brought many riches in the afterlife. Vikings were buried or cremated with some of their belongings to take with them to the afterlife. The chiefs and warriors often had ship cremations: their bodies were placed on their ships with their belongings and then set fire to and sent to sea.

Activities

1. Viking burial recount

Give children information about Viking burial customs and ask them to make notes about what happened at Viking burials and cremations. As a class, think about what they might see, hear, smell and touch at a Viking burial ceremony of a great Viking warrior. Children should discuss ideas with their partners before writing an idea on a post-it and sticking it on a large sheet of paper. Following this, edit the ideas as a class using these criteria:

- Is this unlikely?
- Is this possible?
- Is this certain?

Ask children to use these reflections and ideas to write a first person recount as if they were at a burial. You could extend this activity by asking children to write from different people's point of view, for example: the wife of the deceased; the friend who survived the battle, the child of the deceased or a villager.

2. Comparison activity

Using their knowledge of the Ancient Egyptian civilisation ask children to compare burial customs of the Viking and Egyptian societies.

Egyptian and Viking burial customs	
Similarities	**Differences**
They were buried with their riches	Egyptians were embalmed and buried
They believed in an afterlife	

Children could extend this beyond these two cultures and look at other civilisations they have studied. Children could begin to think about the impact of their beliefs on their day-to-day lives.

Who was Beowulf?

Beowulf was written around the tenth century CE but it describes the adventures and battles of a great warrior from Norway or Sweden who lived 500 years previously. It is not known how much of the story is based on truth, although some of the people in the poem did exist but it is one of the oldest pieces of British literature to have survived. There is only one copy of the manuscript which is kept in the British Library in London.

Activities

1. *Beowulf and death*

Recalling the children's knowledge of burial customs look at the extract from the translation of Beowulf that follows and scrutinise it as a source of information to support what they already know about death and burial in the time of the Vikings.

Ask the children to annotate the information in the text and discuss how this supports what they already know as well as highlighting any new or conflicting information.

Children could use three different colour pens to annotate the text for fact, opinion and fiction.

Shield died at his fated hour,
went to God still strong.
His people carried him to the sea,
which was his last request.
In the harbor stood
a well-built ship,
icy but ready for the sea.
They laid Shield there,
propped him against the mast
surrounded by gold
and treasure from distant lands.
I've never heard
of a more beautiful ship,
filled with shields, swords,
and coats of mail, gifts
to him for his long trip.
No doubt he had a little more
than he did as a child
when he was sent out,
a naked orphan in an empty boat.
Now he had a golden banner
high over his head, was,
sadly by a rich people,
given to the sea.
The wisest alive can't tell
where a death ship goes.

2. *Viking opulence*

It would be helpful if the children had read the story of Beowulf or seen the animation prior to this activity. Ask children to use the extracts from Beowulf to look at how Beowulf was rewarded with riches and treasures after his valiant battle with Grendel. What can this tell us about how warriors were seen in the eyes of nobles?

Then it was ordered
that Herot be decorated.
Many there were,
men and women, who
prepared that guest-hall.
Gold ornaments shone,
wondrous sights on the
walls, for people to look at.

The king ordered eight
horses with gold-plaited
bridles led into the hall.
On one sat a saddle inlaid
with jewels –

Hrothgar gave horses and
weapons, telling Beowulf to
enjoy them well.

Critique Beowulf as a source of evidence by asking the following questions:

- When was it written?
- Who wrote it?
- Why was it written?
- Who was the intended audience?
- How likely is it that the poem is based on true events?
- Which parts of the poem could be true? Which are true? And which are definitely not true?

WHO WERE THE NORMANS?

A little bit of knowledge . . .

The Normans invaded England in 1066 and came from Northern France and were descended from Vikings. They lived in wattle and daub houses but following their invasion of Britain they built magnificent castles to protect their land such as Windsor Castle; by the end of the Norman rule there were numerous castles throughout Britain. William the Conqueror starting building the Tower of London which was significant because it sent a message to any potential invaders that he was a powerful king and that London was his domain. The Normans were skilled craftsmen and constructed many buildings that are still standing in Britain today. The Norman invasion saw a change in the way that Britain was ruled – for the first time there was a king who had absolute power over the whole country. This was a huge change for the country as previously earls and barons had also had some power but now the King's word was the law.

How did the Normans decide who should be king?

When the English King Edward the Confessor died on 5 January 1066 there were no formal procedures in place to decide who the successor would be. The Witan (the council equivalent), had to make the decision and they had four candidates to choose from.

Activities

1. Who's the king?

Ask children to decide who they think should have been the rightful king and why.

Edgar the Atheling	Harold Godwinson
• grandson of Edmund Ironside • direct descendant of Alfred the Great • the rightful heir to Edward the Confessor but only 10 years old when Edward died. • he did not have the support of the Witan • he did not have wealth or power	• his sister was married to Edward the Confessor • was the Earl of Wessex and was considered to be one of the most powerful nobles • he was very wealthy • had once been an advisor to Edward the confessor. • had been a good leader and fighter • some of his family members were on the Witan

William, Duke of Normandy	Harold Hadrada
• Edward the Confessor had lived in Normandy • was a distant cousin of Edward the Confessor • claimed that Edward had promised the throne to him • Normandy had acted as a refuge in times of trouble as well as being strong trading partners with England • many Norman advisors in court had been brought over by Edward	• was a Viking • before Edward seized the throne it had been promised to Harold Hadrada and he wished to claim it back

Ask children to do more research on these people and make their decisions; justifying their reasons and thinking about what the impact may have been. How would history have been different?

2. *Norman kings*

Provide children with a list of Norman kings and remind them that the first Norman king: William the Conqueror was the first official King of England.

Timeline activity: arrange the Norman kings in chronological order on a washing line.

	Empress Matilda (1141)
William II, Rufus (1087–1100)	**Henry I, Beauclerc (1100–35)**
Richard I, the Lionheart (1189–99)	**John, Lackland (1199–1216)**
William I, the Conqueror (1066–87)	**Stephen (1135–54)**
Edward II (1307–27)	**Edward I, Longshanks (1272–1307)**
Henry III (1216–72)	**Henry II, Curtmantle (1154–89)**
Richard II (1377–99	**Edward III (1327–77)**

This activity could be developed into a research activity by asking children to find out more information about each ruler as well as some key events from the time. These can then be added to their timeline.

Who was William the Conqueror?

William the Conqueror ordered the writing of the Domesday book which contained everything that was owned by Britain at that time. This has been a useful source of information for historians and tells us much about what life was like during Norman times.

Activities

1. Significant people: William the Conqueror

Provide children with an enquiry question: What was life like under William the Conqueror's rule in Norman times? They should use the four sources to help them begin their enquiry, thinking about: what life was like during the rule of William the Conqueror and how he made an impact on the lives of people of Britain.

Source 1: A description of William the Conqueror by William of Jumieges

William, Duke of Normandy, never allowed himself to be deterred from any enterprise because of the labour it entailed. He was strong in body and tall in stature. He was moderate in drinking, for he deplored drunkenness in all men. In speech he was fluent and persuasive, being skilled at all times in making clear his will. He followed the Christian discipline in which he had been brought up from childhood, and whenever his health permitted he regularly attended Christian worship each morning and at the celebration of mass.

Source 2: An extract from the Anglo-Saxon chronicle

He (William) made large forests for the deer, and passed laws, so that whoever killed a hart or a hind should be blinded. The rich complained and the poor murmured, but the king was so strong that he took no notice of them.

Source 3: A list of some of the Motte and Bailey castles in Britain (there are many more)

- Buckingham, Bucks
- Carleon, Gwent, Wales
- Cardiff, S Glamorgan, Wales
- Dudley, West Midlands
- Farnham, Surrey
- Gloucester, Glos
- Hastings, E. Sussex
- Monfichet, London
- Oakham, Rutland
- Pickering, N Yorks
- Saffron Walden, Essex
- Thetford, Norfolk
- Wakefield, W Yorks
- Windsor, Berks
- York, N Yorks

Source 4: An account by the Bishop of Hereford of the compilation of the Domesday book

They... made a survey of all England; of the lands in each of the counties; of the possessions of each of the magnates, their lands, their habitations, their men, both bond and free, living in huts or with their own houses or land; of ploughs, horses and other animals; of the services and payments due from each and every estate.

After these investigators came others who were sent to unfamiliar counties to check the first description and to denounce any wrong-doers to the king. And the land was troubled with many calamities arising from the gathering of the royal taxes.

2. *Domesday book*

Look at the extract below from the Domesday book and ask children to highlight any words that they know in one colour and words they do not know in another colour. Explain that the Domesday book was written in Latin and that this is a translation.

Extract from the Domesday book

Fredrebruge Hundred and half Glorestorp. Godwin, a freeman, held it. Two carucates of land in the time of king Edward. Then and afterwards 8 villains; now 3. Then and afterwards 3 bordars; now 5. At all times 3 serfs, and 30 acres of meadow. At all times 2 carucates in demesne. Then half a carucate of the men, and now. Woods for 8 swine, and 2 mills. Here are located 13 socmen, of 40 acres of land. When it was received there were 2 r.,' now 1. At all times 8 swine, then 20 sheep, and it is worth 60 shillings.

There is situated there, in addition, one berewick, as the manor of Heuseda. In the time of king Edward, 1 carucate of land; then and afterwards 7 villains, now 5. At all times 12 bordars, and 3 serfs, and 40 acres of meadow; 1 mill. Woods for 16 swine and

> 1 salt pond and a half Then 1 r., and now and 14 swine, 30 sheep, and 50 goats. In this berewick are located 3 socmen, of 10 acres of land, and it is worth 30 shillings. The two manors have 2 leagues in length and 4 firlongs in breadth. Whosoever is tenant there, returns 12 pence of the twenty shillings of geld.

Children can try to use their inference skills to decipher the meaning of any unknown words before using books and web sources to carry out research to find out what the words that they are unfamiliar with mean – can they see similarities with the word we use today? Children can then use this information to create a glossary of terms.

The collection of information for the Domesday book was crucial as this was the first time that there had been a king of the whole country and this book recorded what was owned and ruled by William the Conqueror.

How did the Normans conquer Britain?

William the Conqueror became King of England in 1066 after a fierce battle with Harold Hadrada for the crown. The Battle of Hastings lasted only six hours and at first it seemed that Harold would win easily as the Normans were unable to break the wall that his men had made with their shields. However, when the English troops thought the Normans were retreating, they chased them down the hill. But the Normans turned and used this as an opportunity to break through their weakened defences and cut them down. As William the Conqueror was victorious he became the new King of England.

Activities

1. The Bayeaux tapestry as a source of information

The Bayeux tapestry is embroidery that tells the story of the Norman invasion in 1066; it was commissioned by William's half brother who wished to commemorate his brother's success. It is 50cm tall and over 70m long and resides in Bayeaux in Normandy, France. There is not an equivalent Anglo-Saxon record of the battle

– discuss with the children what this tells us about the tapestry as a source of information. Ask children to look at images of the tapestry (freely available from web sources) and answer the following questions:

- Which figures do you think are the Normans and which are the Anglo-Saxons? Why?
- What weapons can you see?
- What do you think happened to Harald?
- What words can you see?
- What sorts of ships were used?
- What animals can you see?
- What can you see in the border of the picture?

Children should get as much information as possible from the images before using other sources to support their judgements.

2. *Motte and bailey castles*

The Normans built the first castles in England – these became known as motte and bailey castles; the first one was Windsor Castle which has a motte with several baileys. Using the information below begin by asking children to match the definition with the feature.

Feature	**Definition**
motte	The mound where the castle was built. This had steep sides to stop the enemy from climbing up easily
keep	The lookout or the central strongpoint
bailey	The area at the bottom of the motte where the people lived
moat	A ditch around the castle often filled with water
drawbridge	A bridge that could be closed or opened over the moat to allow access
small, narrow windows	Used for shooting arrows through – harder for enemies to aim at

Following this activity ask children to look at images of some of the motte and bailey castles left in Britain and find and label the features above.

3. *The feudal system*

When William conquered Britain in 1066 he took all the land from the people who owned it and distributed it amongst the barons who had supported his invasion; this led to a feudal system where the king owned all the land; the barons looked after the land and controlled the knights who in turn controlled villeans (peasants) who were like slaves, working the land (see below). This was a medieval class system with all roads leading back to the king who was the overall ruler.

<table>
<tr><td colspan="8">king</td></tr>
<tr><td colspan="4">baron</td><td colspan="4">baron</td></tr>
<tr><td colspan="2">knight</td><td colspan="2">knight</td><td colspan="2">knight</td><td colspan="2">knight</td></tr>
<tr><td>villean</td><td>villean</td><td>villean</td><td>villean</td><td>villean</td><td>villean</td><td>villean</td><td>villean</td></tr>
</table>

Ask children to think about what it would have been like to be one of these people. Give children a title (king, baron, knight or villean) and ask them to research the roles and responsibilities for their person – what was expected of them? Ask the children to write a recount. Following this ask children to think about why they think the king wanted this system in place.

Comparing Vikings, Anglo-Saxons and Normans

Pupils have learnt about the Vikings, Anglo-Saxons and Normans. Now ask them to compare them. This can be done in categories as outlined below:

	Vikings	Anglo-Saxons	Normans
Daily life			
Battles			
Role of women			
Buildings			
Rights and laws			
Travel			
Leaders			

Don't forget to update your class timeline to reflect the new periods in history that you have learnt about.

CHAPTER 5
The Tudors and the Stuarts

The activities in this chapter provide ways in which children can begin to understand the Tudor reign and what life was like during that time. The Tudor dynasty was of Welsh origin and was descended from Prince Rhys Ap Tewdwr. The Tudor period was an exciting time and some major historical events occurred including The Battle of Bosworth which signalled the end of the War of the Roses; the six wives of Henry VIII and the break with the Pope and the Church of Rome. This resulted in Henry VIII being head of the Church of England. There were also two female queens during the Tudor reign: Mary I and Elizabeth I. The death of Elizabeth I saw an end to Tudor rule as she had no heirs and made way for the beginning of the Stuart rule.

The Stuart kings were the first kings who ruled both England and Scotland: King James VI of Scotland was also King James I of England. The Stuart period was relatively short (1603–1714) and volatile; being remembered as a time of plague, fire and war.

This chapter will provide activities which will help to develop children's understanding of both the Tudor and Stuart periods as well as develop some key historical skills such as enquiry, using inference and developing overall understanding of people, places and time.

WHO WERE THE TUDORS?

A little bit of knowledge . . .

The first Tudor in the dynasty was Henry VII who was called Henry Tudor and defeated Richard III at the Battle of Bosworth in 1485. He kept the crown until 1509 when his son Henry VIII took the crown. Henry VII's first son was called Arthur and was married to Catherine of Aragon who later married his brother Henry VIII after his death. Henry VIII is possibly one of the most famous and notorious monarchs due to his many wives and rumoured infidelity as well as his impact on the lives of the British people. The Tudor period is remembered as a time of great religious change and reform as well as exploration.

The six monarchs in the Tudor period were:

Henry VII	1485–1509
Henry VIII	1509–1547
Edward VI	1547–1553
Lady Jane Grey de facto monarch	nine days in 1553
Mary I	1553–1558
Elizabeth I	1558–1603

Key vocabulary

Reformation, beheaded, execution, treason, The Tower of London, heretics (the name for those who believed in a different religion to the sovereign), exploration, Shakespeare, Spanish Armada

Who were significant figures in Tudor times?

Many of the most famous names in royal history lived during the Tudor period. It was a turbulent time, and the people and their actions still impact on our lives today.

Activities

1. *Matching game*

Ask pupils to match up significant Tudors with what they are remembered for. Provide students with cards outlining significant information about famous Tudors and another set with names on. Children to match them up – this should generate a useful discussion.

Shakespeare	Famous playwright
Mary Tudor	First female monarch
Elizabeth I	Last reigning monarch in the Tudor dynasty. No heirs to the throne.
Sir Walter Raleigh	Famous Tudor explorer
Sir Francis Drake	Defeated the Spanish Armada who had come to England to overthrow Elizabeth I.
Catherine of Aragon	First wife of Henry VIII: provided an heir to the throne: Mary I
Anne Boleyn	Her marriage to Henry VIII resulted in huge religious change for England. Provided an heir to the throne: Elizabeth I
William Tyndale	Translated the bible into English
Jane Seymour	Henry's third wife. Provided an heir to the throne: Edward VI who ruled for 6 years until his death at age 16.

Now that children have some basic information about these significant Tudors ask them to work in groups and find out more about one of them before sharing with the rest of the class. Encourage children to discuss which Tudor was the most significant and why – which one had the biggest impact on our lives today?

2. *Significance timeline*
Following on from the above activity ask children to create a significance timeline. Provide them with cards stating: Name of person; significant event; date significant event occurred for example:

William Tyndale	Translated the bible into English	1522CE

They should then organise these in chronological order on a timeline (a washing line and pegs works well) to demonstrate when each event occurred; this should also help them to see which events were happening during the same period of time as well as the time periods that these events spanned. This could be done as a whole class activity or in groups. Provide the children with some discussion questions such as:

- What was the impact of this event at the time?
- What impact remains for people living today?
- How may history have been altered if _______ had not occurred?

Who was Henry VIII and why do we remember him?
Henry VIII was born in Greenwich on 28 June 1491 and went on to be King of England; inheriting the throne from his brother, Prince Arthur. He is most remembered for having numerous wives however, he was also instrumental in changing the religion of Britain from Catholicism to Protestantism which had a significant impact on the lives of the British people both in Tudor times and today. He was also father to two of the most significant monarchs in Tudor history: Mary Tudor, as she was the first female monarch and Queen Elizabeth I who reigned for more than 40 years and whose death signalled the end of the Tudor dynasty as she had no heirs to the throne.

Activity
1. *Discussion cube: Henry's wives*
Provide children with information about each wife. You can add images if required.

Catherine of Aragon	**Anne Boleyn**
Daughter of the rulers of Spain Born 16 December 1485 Married to Henry's brother: Prince Arthur Married Henry in 1509 They had one daughter who survived (Mary) and a son who died Marriage dissolved in 1533	She was at court Born between 1500–1509 Married Henry in 1533 They had one daughter (Elizabeth) She was executed in 1536
Jane Seymour She was at court Born in 1508 Married Henry in 1536 They had a son (Edward) Died in 1537	**Anne of Cleves** Marriage of convenience to build alliances with France Born in 1515 Married Henry in 1540 (January–July) Marriage dissolved in 1540
Kathryn Howard First cousin of Anne Boleyn Lady in waiting to Anne of Cleves Born: 1521–1525 Married Henry in 1540 Executed in 1542	**Katherine Parr** She was known to the family Born in 1512 Married Henry in 1543 She outlived Henry

Use a net to make a cube with each side having the name of one of Henry VIII's wives written on it. When children have thrown the dice another child can ask them questions about their wife such as:

- When was I born?
- Did I have children?
- How long was I married to Henry?
- Which wife was I?
- When did my marriage end?

This could generate a discussion about who was the most significant wife and why. Children could be encouraged to ask and answer questions such as: Which wife influenced Henry the most? Which wife do you think Henry loved the most? Why did women want to marry Henry? If Henry had not died do you think his marriage to Katherine Parr would have lasted?

What can we find out about Tudor times from looking at artefacts?
Artefacts are items that can help us understand more about the past. They are a useful source of information as they help us explain what life was like in the past. Artefacts are one of the ways that historians can build up a picture of what it was like in the past.

Activities

1. Tudor artefacts

Provide children with photographs of artefacts from Tudor times and photographs of items from today (some of which should also have been common in Tudor Times). Working in groups, children can create a Venn diagram using two large hoops. They can use this Venn to sort the objects into: items from Tudor times; items used today and items used in both Tudor and modern times. Images are available online and could include (but are not limited to):

- eating and drinking items – utensils, jugs etc
- purses
- tools
- writing implements.

The item may have originally been designed for use in Tudor times but may be used today for a slightly different purpose. The key aspect here is the children's discussions not whether they place items in the correct section of the Venn diagram.

2. *Rich and poor Tudors*

Give children enquiry questions to investigate:

- What was life like for poor Tudors?
- What was life like for rich Tudors?
- What were the reasons for the differences?

Divide the children into groups and ask each group to investigate one of the following areas before sharing their ideas with the rest of the class. This can be done by organising the children into mixed groups with an 'expert' from each area who will share their knowledge. Children can use their information to write an account of what life was like for poor and rich Tudors focusing on the areas studied before making comparisons.

home	work	diet	family
entertainment	roles	health	religion

What was life like for women in Tudor times?

Tudor times were significant for women as there were two female monarchs who were able to reign in their own right as their father had done. This was the first time this had ever happened. The fact that Elizabeth I made a conscious decision not to marry meant that she was seen as a ruler in her own right. This was thought to be intentional – Elizabeth did not want the people of Britain to think that she was being guided by a man.

Activity

True or false

Provide pupils with statements about the lives and habits of women in Tudor times. Some are true and some are false. Pupils should decide, justifying their opinions.

True statements	False statements
Unmarried girls would have to stay at home with their parents and spin yarn (this is where the word spinster comes from)	Girls had to marry and look after the husbands
Girls could marry at the age of twelve	Girls had to stay with their families until they were 15 before they could marry
Families did not think it was worth sending girls to school as they could learn all the household chores from their mothers	Girls were forbidden from attending school
Women could be punished for nagging, gossiping or telling someone off. Punishments included the ducking stool and wearing an iron mask which would hold the tongue down	Women were forbidden from gossiping and nagging and those who did had their tongues removed
Elizabethan women wanted to have white skin, blue eyes, ruby red lips and fair hair	Elizabethan women wanted to have white skin, brown eyes, red lips and red hair
To make their lips red women used to wear lipstick made from crushed beetles	To make their lips red women used to wear lipstick made from lambs blood
To have sparkly eyes women used to use belladonna (a poisonous drug made from deadly nightshade)	To have sparkly eyes women would use men's urine
Elizabethan women considered bathing unhealthy so they covered up smell with perfume	Elizabethan women considered cleanliness important and liked to bath regularly

What happened if you committed a crime in Tudor times?

There were no police in Tudor times but crimes were severely punished; many Tudors faced the death penalty simply for stealing a small amount of money. Some historians believe that more than 70,000 people were executed during Henry VIII's reign – most of these were beheadings and the heads would be displayed on London Bridge as a warning to others of the penalty for committing crimes.

Activities

1. Crime and punishment

In Tudor times punishments were severe and often resulted in death. Many crimes came with particular consequences. Show children a list of punishments that were commonly used in Tudor times and ask them to think what crimes may have been committed to deserve a punishment of this kind.

Beheading Head is cut off (usually in front of a crowd)	**Hanging** Hung from a rope around the neck until dead (usually in front of a crowd)
Stocks Large wooden board which lock the feet and/or hands in place	**Burnt at the stake** Tied to a large wooden post in a bonfire and set alight
Brank/scold's bridle A large metal brace worn on the head	**Whipping** Tied to a post and hit repeatedly with a leather whip
Limbs severed Legs or arms cut off (with no anaesthetic or pain killers!)	**Drunkards cloak** A tub or barrel worn on the body with holes for the arms and legs
Ducking stool A chair fastened to the end of a pole used to plunge people into water	**Stretching** Tied to a rack and legs and arms stretched by pulleys and levers

When children have had a discussion about potential crimes that could have matched these punishments show them the answers below:

Punishment	Detail	Crime
Beheading	Head is cut off (usually in front of a crowd)	Serious crimes such as murder, speaking against the royal family or the church. This was generally for rich and important people
Stocks	Large wooden board which lock the feet and/or hands in place	For small crimes such as swearing and being homeless (a vagrant)
Brank/scold's bridle	A large metal brace worn on the head	For women who gossiped
Limbs severed	Legs or arms cut off (with no anaesthetic or pain killers!)	For stealing (more valuable items)
Ducking stool	A chair fastened to the end of a pole used to plunge people into water	For women who were accused of being a witch
Hanging	Hung from a rope around the neck until dead (usually in front of a crowd)	Serious crimes such as murder, speaking against the royal family or the church. This was generally for poor people
Burnt at the stake	Tied to a large wooden post in a bonfire and set alight	Serious crimes such as murder, speaking against the royal family or the church. This was generally for women

Punishment	Detail	Crime
Whipping	Tied to a post and hit repeatedly with a leather whip	For stealing (food and cheaper items)
Drunkards cloak	A tub or barrel worn on the body with holes for the arms and legs	For being seen drunk in public
Stretching	Tied to a rack and legs and arms stretched by pulleys and levers	A form of torture to get people to talk

Ask children to think about how this relates to the way crimes are punished today. What are the differences? Why do you think this has changed? (Remember that there was no police)

Ask children to think about why crime was still so prevalent even though the punishments were so severe? What does this tell you about life in Tudor times?

2. ***Excuses excuses!***
Ask children to take on the role of deciding who deserves to be punished and how. This could be done as a role play with some children taking on the roles of the accused and others the deciders.

Name	Crime accused of committing	Defence
John Thomas	Drunkenness	My third child had been born and I was in the inn with my friends. I had one or two cups of ale and felt very happy. I walked home and started singing merry songs because I was so happy.

Name	Crime accused of committing	Defence
Henry Dunne	Gossip	My wife told me that Joan Edwards from the village was cooking strange things in her house, never spoke to anyone and did not have a family. She had a strange mark on her arm; all I did was tell my friends but they went home and told their wives.
Nicholas Chambers	Speaking against the church	I have always been a Catholic and I intend to stay that way no matter what the King says.
Joan Edwards	Witchcraft	I am just a quiet lady who keeps myself to myself; I do not want to mix with people in this village as they are all loose-tongued. I am happy staying in with my cats.
Richard Black	Vagrancy	I have been unable to find work and am down on my luck. I have nowhere to live but am happy to do any work and am an honest man.
Alice Dunne	Gossip	All I did was tell my husband that I though Joan was a witch. She never speaks to anyone and spends all day in her house with her cats and strange smells come from her home.
Margaret John	Treason	All I did was say that I could not believe the King was marrying so soon after the death of Queen Anne. He should concentrate on running the country and not running after young girls.

Make it clear that the children need to be able to justify their decisions based on the reasons that Tudors may have given and not ones that we may have today.

3. *Analysing sources*

There are some crimes and their punishments which are well documented in history but may seem unfair and difficult to comprehend by today's standards. Perhaps one of the most well known Tudor crimes was the beheading of King Henry's wife Anne Boleyn as this was the first public execution of an English Queen.

Using the sources below, ask children to think about what was said by Anne Boleyn and how this compared to the crime she was accused of.

Source 1: Anne's crimes

Anne was accused of conspiring to murder the King by having relationships with men who would do her bidding for her.

Source 2: Anne's reasons or excuses

Account written by Lancelot de Carles

I do not say that I have always borne towards the King the humility which I owed him, considering his kindness and the great honour he showed me and the great respect he always paid me; I admit too, that often I have taken it into my head to be jealous of him... But may God be my witness if I have done him any other wrong.

Source 3: Anne's words before she was executed

Account written by Edward Hall

Anne was beheaded on 19 May 1536 at 8am

Good Christian people, I am come hither to die, for according to the law, and by the law I am judged to die, and therefore I will speak nothing against it. I am come hither to accuse no man, nor to speak anything of that, whereof I am accused and condemned to die, but I pray God save the King and send him long to reign over you, for a gentler nor a more merciful prince was there never: and to me he was ever a good, a gentle and sovereign lord. And if any person will meddle of my cause, I require them to judge the best. And thus I take my leave of the world and of you all, and I heartily desire you all to pray for me. O Lord have mercy on me, to God I commend my soul.

When analysing the sources ask children to do the following:

- Think about where the sources are from: who wrote them, when and why.
- Question the information they have, for example: why did Anne still appear loyal to the King even though he had sentenced her to death (the jury was made up of loyal supporters of King Henry and close friends and family members of the King – Anne did not stand a chance of being found not guilty!)
- Think about what this tells us about what life was like in Tudor times.
- Perhaps children could do more research on the trial of Anne Boleyn and find out a bit more about her – can they investigate her trial in more detail?

WHO WERE THE STUARTS?

A little bit of knowledge...

The Stuart period began in England in 1603 and ended in 1714. The death of Queen Elizabeth I, without an heir, resulted in James I becoming King of England as well as King of Scotland. The Stuart era had many events that we remember today such as the gunpowder plot, the great plague, the great fire of London and exploration to America. This was a puritan era and many activities were banned such as gambling, cock-fighting and even Christmas. Religion was contentious at this time and this resulted in a civil war between crown and parliament (also known as the Cavaliers and the Roundheads). There was much bloodshed and the war ended with the execution of King Charles I by Oliver Cromwell. Cromwell's rule was short-lived as the restoration of the crown followed soon after with William and Mary of Orange ascending to the throne.

The British Empire had been expanding and continued to do so. Imported items included sugar and coffee from East Indies, tea from India and slaves from Africa.

Key vocabulary

Puritans, trade, Stuarts, exploration, gunpowder plot, parliament, plague, Fire of London, acts of union.

What was the gunpowder plot?

The gunpowder plot in 1605 was an attempt to assassinate King James I of England. The assassins were a group of English Catholics led by Robert Catesby. The plot was to blow up the House of Lords during the state opening of parliament on 5th November but the group were unsuccessful as their plot was revealed and they were caught. Guy Fawkes was discovered with the gunpowder and along with eight other plotters was sentenced to be hung, drawn and quartered.

Activities

1. *Gunpowder lyrics*

Read aloud some of the poems from this time linked to the gunpowder plot such as 'The Fifth of November' (*English Folk Verse 1870*) and ask children to create a wordscape of interesting words and vocabulary from the poems – this could then be used to create a wordle on the computer or a haiku poem. What do the words of the poem tell us about how people felt about the event? What was public feeling at the time? Do you think everyone felt this way or were there some people who may have felt differently? Why do you think this was? Look at other sources of evidence to ensure children have a full picture of both sides of the story. What drove this group of people to act in this way?

2. *Source square*

Place a picture of Guy Fawkes in the middle of a square and ask children to think about who he was, what he was famous for, what they infer about his character from the picture. This activity could be enhanced and developed by providing each group with alternative images of Guy Fawkes, portraying him in different ways. Think about who produced the image, when it was produced and who else is in the image. They could also think about whether he would have been as famous had the assassination attempt happened in today's times. What would his punishment have been had he committed this crime today?

What do we know about the great fire of London from the diary of Samuel Pepys?

The great fire of London was catastrophic to the city of London, destroying over 13,000 homes which equated to most of the population of London. It also destroyed St Paul's Cathedral and over 85 parish churches. It is hard to know for sure how many people died as the deaths of poor people were not usually recorded and the fire was so hot and burned for so long that many bodies may have been cremated. The fire started in a bakery in Pudding Lane owned by Thomas Farriner and burned for four whole days before it was brought under control.

Activities

1. *Diary work*

Read an extract from Samuel Pepys diary and analyse the text in groups. Children could have the same or different extracts.

Extract 1: About the great fire of London: 2 September 1666

So down [I went], with my heart full of trouble, to the Lieutenant of the Tower, who tells me that it began this morning in the King's baker's house in Pudding Lane, and that it hath burned St. Magnus's Church and most part of Fish Street already. So I rode down to the waterside,... and there saw a lamentable fire.... Everybody endeavouring to remove their goods, and flinging into the river or bringing them into lighters that lay off; poor people staying in their houses as long as till the very fire touched them, and then running into boats, or clambering from one pair of stairs by the waterside to another. And among other things, the poor pigeons, I perceive, were loth to leave their houses, but hovered about the windows and balconies, till they some of them burned their wings and fell down.

Extract 2: About the plague: 7 June 7 1665

...it being the hottest day that ever I felt in my life, and it is confessed so by all other people the hottest they ever knew in England in the beginning of June – we to the New Exchange and there drunk whey; with much entreaty, getting it for our money, and would not be entreated to let us have one glasse more. ...

This day, much against my Will, I did in Drury-lane see two or three houses marked with a red cross upon the doors, and 'Lord have mercy upon us' writ there – which was a sad sight to me, being the first of that kind that to my remembrance I ever saw. It put me into an ill conception of myself and my smell, so that I was forced to buy some roll tobacco to smell to and chaw – which took away the apprehension.

Extract 3: About the coronation 23 April 23 1661

The King in his robes, bare headed, which was very fine. And after all had placed themselfs – there was a sermon and the service. And then in the Quire at the high altar he passed all the ceremonies of the Coronacion – which, to my very great grief, I and most of the Abbey could not see. The crowne being put upon his head, a great shout begun. And he came forth to the Throne and there passed more ceremonies: as, taking the oath and having things read to him by the Bishopp, and his lords (who put on their capps as soon as the King put on his Crowne) and Bishopps came and kneeled before him.

Look for the following:

- What can be understood about the period from the extract?
- What can be inferred about the time?
- What else is there to know? Children can use this as a basis to explore and answer their own questions.

Children could also write their own diary extract and stain it with tea for that authentic aged appearance.

2. *Painting work*

Look at paintings from the time of the great fire of London. Cover up half the image and ask the children to draw the rest of it. You could also use the same image to play I spy. Using a viewfinder ask the children to look at a section of the image in depth – what does this image tell us about the fire? How were people able to escape? How did the infrastructure of London at that time exacerbate the fire? How much of London was affected? What was used to put out the fire? Where did it start? Why did it spread so quickly?

3. *Who or what was to blame for the great fire?*

There are many reasons why this fire has been named 'the great fire'. Ask children to explore the facts below and think about who or what was to blame for the fire.

The bakery	Houses
Thomas Farriner's maid did not put out the fire properly and when it overwhelmed her she tried to climb out of the window but was not successful and died.	Houses in London at that time were made of wood. The wood was very dry as it had been a long, hot summer.
Infrastructure	**Wind**
London was a large city that had grown quickly – people lived in close proximity and houses were very close together.	There was a strong wind which fanned the flames and caused the fire to spread more rapidly.
The Lord Mayor	**Charles II**
The Mayor of London did not act quickly enough to organise the troops to put out the fire, as he hoped it would die out.	He planned to create fire breaks which meant knocking down buildings that were undamaged but prevented the fire from spreading any further.

Ask children to sort the facts above into an order, considering which ones had the biggest impact on the great fire of London. Who or what was the most to blame for the fire being so severe?

Ask children to think about how the fire may have benefited the people of London, for example:

- Charles II was seen as a hero as he did not evacuate and was instrumental in stopping the fire from spreading.
- Evacuation from London meant that people settled elsewhere, easing the burden on the city's population.
- Christopher Wren (the architect) was asked to rebuild London and is now famous for building St Paul's Cathedral.
- The city slums and filthy, disease ridden streets were simply destroyed eradicating plague and rats.

Who were significant figures in Stuart times?

Stuart times were eventful; there was exploration and significant events such as the plague and the great fire of London. It was also a time of unrest and political uncertainty.

Activities

1. Who am I?

Give children statements about a figure – they have to guess who it is from the clues.

Figure	Clues
James I	My reign was 1603–1625 I was the great grandson of Henry VII I was born in Scotland My mother was Mary Queen of Scots
Charles I	My reign was 1625–1649 I was born in Scotland My father was James I I fought against parliament leading to a civil war I was executed
Guy Fawkes	I hatched a plot to overthrow the King I was a Catholic I was angry because we were treated badly I was hung, drawn and quartered for my act of treason

Figure	Clues
Oliver Cromwell	I was the Lord Protector of the former England, now known as the Commonwealth. I was not popular at home or abroad I was ruthless and had many people killed I did not like Irish Catholics I set up colonies in Jamaica and the West Indies
Samuel Pepys	I wrote a famous diary I lived in London I was a member of parliament I lived through the civil war and two disasters
Pocahontas	I was a native American I travelled to England with my husband John Rolf I changed my name to Rebecca Rolf My family stayed behind and worked with colonists in Jamestown.
Charles II	My father was Charles I I helped stop the fire of London and rebuild the city

2. *Timeline*

Using the information above ask the children to work in groups and research the lives of the people highlighted; focusing on key dates and events. When they have done this ask them to make cards that can be placed on a timeline; outlining significant events, when they happened and the significant people involved. This could be a layered timeline which illustrates how these events, people and times were linked.

Would you rather have been a Tudor or Stuart?

Ask children to work in two groups and assign each one as a Tudor or a Stuart (you could make this a bit more fun by giving them a token to signal which time they belonged to such as a hat or a ruff). Children to create a mind map of the knowledge they have of each period of time (they could access additional knowledge using sources if they have any gaps) and they then have to create an argument as to why it was better to be a Stuart or a Tudor.

CHAPTER 6
The Victorians

The activities in this chapter provide ways in which children can begin to understand the Victorian era and its impact on their lives today. It was a period of rapid change and development which helped secure Britain's place in the wider world as a leader in invention and industry.

This chapter will provide activities which will help to develop children's understanding of the Victorians as well as developing some key historical skills such as enquiry, using inference and developing overall understanding of people, places and time.

These activities will include topics such as: The British Empire, Queen Victoria, industrial revolution, Victorian childhood, significant Victorians and famous inventions as well as covering areas such as social class and philanthropy. These should help children to understand the legacy of the Victorian period.

WHO WERE THE VICTORIANS?

A little bit of knowledge . . .

The Victorian era takes its name from Queen Victoria, who at the time of publication, is the longest reigning monarch in British history. She was Queen of Britain from 1837 to 1901. At that time Britain ruled the British Empire which meant that not only did Queen Victoria rule Britain but she was also Empress of India; and ruled Canada and other smaller countries such as Jamaica. Travel routes also improved during this period which meant a huge growth in migration and immigration as well as trade between empire states.

At this time of change the industrial revolution saw Britain change or develop from a land of villages, farms and towns into a country of heavily populated cities which were centres for industry. Whilst these changes brought great wealth to the country there was also extreme poverty and the divisions in social class were vast.

Key vocabulary

industry, Empire, colonisation, migration, trade, urbanisation, social class, inventions, legacy, revolution, philanthropy (social reform), Victorians

What happened during the reign of Queen Victoria?

Queen Victoria was the monarch of Great Britain and Ireland from 20 June 1837 until her death on 22 January 1901. She was only 18 when she inherited the throne so she had a lot to learn about being queen. Victoria married her first cousin, Prince Albert of Saxe-Goburg and Gotha (this is Germany today) and they had nine children. Family and family values were very important to Queen Victoria and she is often seen posing with her large family in formal portraits. Victoria reigned for 63 years and seven months and she saw many changes during this time; she was not always a popular monarch, however, due to the length of her reign and the legacy of this time she remains a key monarch in history.

Activities

1. ***Key events from the Victorian era***

Provide students with nine key events (dates removed) from the Victorian era and ask them to arrange them chronologically. This should generate a discussion about what life was like and the impact the events would have had on different classes of people.

Nine key events:

1834 Slavery banned in British colonies
1837–67 Isambard Kingdom Brunel builds the London to Bristol railway for the Great Western Railway (GWR)

1851	First telegraph cable laid across the English channel
1863	First underground railway between Paddington and Farringdon Street
1870	Married Women's Property Act – allowed to keep money for their own use
1876	Victoria named Empress of India
1877	Telephones invented by Scottish scientist Alexander Graham Bell become available
1891	Education made free for every child
1901	Population of London reaches 6.6 million

Extension activity: children to decide on which event was the most significant and rank them in order to create a diamond shape (diamond nine activity).

2. *Using visual literacy to form and justify opinions*

Choose four contrasting images of Queen Victoria (there are many available on the internet) and ask children to work in a group to answer the following questions:

- Is it a painting or a photograph?
- Why was it taken/painted?
- What questions would you ask the image?

Then place a picture in the middle of a large sheet of paper and ask children to make notes or write on post-its their responses to the following:

- What can I observe in this image?
- What can I question about this image? (I wonder if…)
- What can I infer? (I think that …because…)

What was the industrial revolution?

The industrial revolution was a major turning point in British history and that of the wider world. The daily lives of Victorians were heavily influenced by this time; new manufacturing processes resulted in major growth from 1760 to sometime between 1820 and 1840. Tools became more efficient and machinery cut down on costs and increased production as did new ways to create energy such as coal and steam.

Activities

2. Comparing the lives of a factory worker and a land worker

Provide pupils with the pen portraits below and ask them to think about what the similarities and differences between these two people's lives would have been. Ask the pupils to think about the impact of the industrial revolution and the growth of industry, cities and railways: was this good for everyone?

Albert: factory worker

Albert is 20 years old, he has worked in the matchstick factory since just before his tenth birthday. He gets up at 5.30am every day, washes in cold water, has a breakfast of warm bread and raspberry jam with eggs from their chickens which his wife has prepared and leaves at 6am to walk a few minutes to the factory at the end of his road. He works all day with one ten minute break and leaves work at 6pm. The factory owner is very cruel – he tries to keep his head down to avoid a beating. When he gets home his back is stiff and he is very tired as he works six and half days a week. His wife has prepared him soup with suet pudding for his supper and he reads his paper by the oil light before going to bed at 9pm.

John: farm hand

John is 20 years old and has worked on the farm since he was six years old. He gets up at 4.30am to collect water to wash in and has stale bread for breakfast before his one hour walk to the farm. He works all day with no break but the farmers' wife gives him a hot meal of stew and warm bread. He leaves the farm at 6pm to begin his one hour journey home. In winter months he is so cold and tired he barely has the energy to get home. Sometimes, if he is lucky, the farmer's wife will give him some spare eggs to take home to his mother but he often goes to bed hungry. He goes to bed at 9pm using a candle to light his dark room.

Extension activity: A railway is to be built in the city which will leave from the city that Albert lives in and go straight past the farm that John works on. Ask the children to debate in role whether they think this will be a good idea or not!

2. *Factory conditions in the Victorian era*

Give pupils a list of facts detailing the acts that were introduced to protect the rights of workers in Victorian Britain. Ask them to compare and contrast the factory acts and think about the implications of lives of factory workers as well as the impact on their family lives and their social lives (if any).

1833 Factory Act

- All children under 11 were to have two hours education a day.
- Children were banned from working in textile factories until they were nine.
- Children aged 9–13 were limited to nine hours a day (48 hours a week).
- Children aged 13–18 were limited to 12 hours a day (69 hours a week).
- Factories were inspected by government inspectors to ensure that factory owners were abiding by the law.

1844 Factory Act

- Children of 8–13 were limited to 6.5 hours a day and this was to be a morning or afternoon shift.
- Workers were entitled to a lunch break.
- Women and young people now worked the same hours (no more than 12 hours a day).
- Ages must be verified by surgeons.
- Accidental death must be reported and investigated.
- Thorough records had to be maintained for government inspectors.
- Safety guards had to be fitted to machines.

What was it like to be a child in Victorian Britain?

The lives of Victorian children were vastly different depending on whether they were rich or poor. Children from poor families had no luxuries, worked long hours and lived in damp, filthy conditions. They had poor diets and due to the filthy and cramped conditions infectious diseases were rife and child mortality was high. In contrast, rich children were usually well fed and well dressed and had an education instead of being made to go and work. They had luxury items such as toys and many even had extravagant pets such as ponies and went on holidays to the seaside.

Activities

1. *Toy makers versus toy breakers*

Show children images of poor children and rich children from the Victorian era and ask them to compare and contrast their lives using the following questions:

- What are the similarities and differences?
- What does the clothing tell us about the period and the conditions they were living in?
- What are they doing in the photograph?
- How are they feeling?
- What can I infer from this image about what their life was like?

Extension activity: Give children half an image or a snapshot of an image and ask them to draw what they think is on the hidden section of the image, using their inference skills.

2. *A wonderful life*

Show children a large number of pictures of Victorian children at work, play, home and education and ask them to categorise them using their own criteria. Children must be able to explain why they have organised the images in this way and justify their reasons.

Extension activity: You could give the pupils different images (one group has home, another work etc) and they do this activity on their table before rotating around the other groups to build up a picture of what Victorian childhood was like.

Some significant Victorians

Lots of changes took place in the Victorian era and many people made important contributions to these changes in society. These people had an impact in different ways and in different areas such as industry, social reform, arts and literature, inventions and women's rights.

Activities

1. Research activity

The following list of famous Victorians could be used in a number of ways to enhance children's understanding of what life was like in Victorian times:

- Choose one person and create an enquiry question such as: How were the lives of children changed by Dr Barnardo? – gather information to answer the question (presentation, role play etc).
- Choose one person and create a fact file on them to present to the class.
- Divide the class into groups and have six different areas to study (arts and literature, industry etc) and ask the children to discuss who they feel was the most significant Victorian and why.
- Choose one Victorian to research in depth – generate questions and do teacher in role or hot seating.

Isambard Kingdom Brunel	John Cadbury	Mary Seacole	Elizabeth Fry
Alexander Graham Bell	Robert Peel	Dr Barnardo	Mary Anning
Michael Faraday	Lord Shaftesbury	Queen Victoria	Alfred Lord Tennyson
Robert Louis Stevenson	Florence Nightingale	Charles Dickens	Joseph Lister
Lewis Carroll	William Morris	Charles Darwin	David Livingston

Some famous Victorian inventions

There were many inventions during this time and so the Great Exhibition of 1851, which took place in Hyde Park in the Crystal Palace, was designed for Great Britain to show off its inventions and industrial changes to the rest of the world. Over 10,000 objects were on display and over half of these came from Britain. Over 6 million people visited the Great Exhibition; it was very successful and the money it raised set up many of the famous museums in London, including the Victoria and Albert Museum, the Science Museum and the Natural History Museum.

Activities

1. Which Victorian invention could you not live without?

Show children a list of significant inventions and ask them to think about which one they could not live without and why.

Bicycles	Postage system and stamps	Rubber tyres	Tarmac	The Metropolitan Police Force
Jelly babies	Barnardo's charity	Antiseptic	Chocolate Easter egg	Telephone
Light bulb	Toilet (and toilet roll)	Cars (and petrol)	Typewriters	Radios
Aspirin	Comics	Ice cream in a tub	Trains and train lines	Bridges
Vacuum cleaners	Sewing machines	X-rays	The Underground	Gliders

Extension activity: Play memory pairs with the inventions and the inventor. For example, Joseph Lister: antiseptic, Alexander Graham Bell: telephone.

2. Following an invention through time

Children to choose an invention and look at how this has developed and evolved throughout the period, for example:

The telephone

1870s	Invented by Alexander Graham Bell
1876	The switchboard was invented – an operator would connect you to whoever you wished to call
1889	Rotary phone invented
1940s	Phones connected to the wall so no need for the operator
1970s	Push button phones
1980s	First mobile phone
1990s	Phones for texting
2013	Present day smartphones – SMS, social media, the web

Extension activity: ask children to create their own invention and have a mini Great Exhibition in school – invite parents in and ask children to apply for patents. This could be the culmination of a Victorian topic.

Additional games or activities:

- Guess what? Describe an invention for the class to guess.
- Draw an invention for the class to guess.
- Hide an object in a bag – children should guess what it is. This game can be adapted so one child describes the hidden object while another draws it on a small whiteboard.

Why was there a need for social reform?

The Victorian age has often been referred to as 'the age of reform'; a time when pressure groups and individual social reformers or philanthropists were particularly active. Social reform was needed as a consequence of industrialisation; there were a number of acts passed during this time which led to a change in society. One of the most recognised philanthropists at the time was the Earl of Shaftesbury who fought for the protection of children employed in factories and mines and then later on, for chimney sweeps. Dr Barnardo was interested in working with homeless and destitute children and built on the work of Lord Shaftesbury. The first Barnardo's home was opened in 1870 in London.

Activities

1. *Charles Dickens*

Show children an extract of a text by Charles Dickens such as *Oliver Twist* (the workhouse scene) and prepare a source square. Place the extract in the middle and draw three squares around it. In the first square ask children to write what they know, in the second what they wonder or think and in the third what they want to find out more about. Use this as a starting point for children to investigate how Charles Dickens wrote about his own experiences and those of his family at this time.

2. *Rights of the child*

Look at the United Nations Rights of a Child document and discuss what the statements mean. Look at the rights and discuss which of these were in place for Victorian children. How have the rights and protection of children changed since Victorian times? Discuss the impact that people such as Charles Dickens and Dr Barnardo had on these changes.

What was the British Empire?

The British Empire included all territories that were ruled by Britain. Queen Victoria was head of the largest empire in history. It controlled almost a quarter of the world's surface and was largely built on trade which made Britain very rich. The most famous part of the British Empire was the East India trading company. The company traded in cotton, silk, dye and tea. Today, Britain is known as a nation of tea drinkers, it was Britain's most popular import during the reign of Queen Victoria. During that time many families emigrated to other parts of the British Empire including Australia, New Zealand, South Africa and Canada. During the 1880s Britain colonised large parts of Africa including Nigeria, Egypt, Uganda and Kenya. Some of the most significant items that were imported are: tea, cotton, jute, tobacco, precious stones, sugar, artefacts (objects d'art), fine cottons, dyes and spices. Cotton was imported and then made into clothing and exported all over the world.

Activities

1. ***Victorian trade***

Imagine that a new product has just been imported to Britain (tea, sugar etc) and it is your job to promote it to the people of Britain – how will you persuade people to buy this product? Think about what they can use it for – how will it enhance their lives? Children could make a poster to advertise their product.

2. ***Who benefited from the British Empire?***

Create a grid, circles or a table for the children and ask them to think about the statements below and then think about what impact each had on Britain and on its colonies, for example

Statements	Impact on Britain	Impact on the colony
A number of raw materials are imported to Britain	Britain benefited from a large supply of raw materials such as rubber, cloth and woollen goods which traders could reuse and sell on to make Britain wealthy	Natural resources were depleted and wealth taken away from the country. Colonies had no chance to develop their own industry and provided cheap labour for Britain
Christianity was the dominant religion in Britain and was introduced in the colonies		
The English language evolved due to colonisation		

Statements	Impact on Britain	Impact on the colony
Britain had sanitation and access to clean water which it took to the colonies.		
Agriculture: food stuffs (chocolate, coffee, bananas)		
Britain built physical infrastructures in Britain and in the colonies. Improved railway links, roads and dams		

CHAPTER 7

World War II and post-war Britain

The activities in this chapter provide ways in which children can begin to understand what life was like in World War II and the impact this event had on post-war Britain. It had a significant impact on the lives of people in Britain but also on the changing roles of women in society.

This chapter will provide activities which will help to develop children's understanding of World War II as well as giving them opportunities to ask questions about the roles of women and children and make comparisons with their lives today.

These activities will include topics such as: evacuation, Battle of Britain, battles and conflicts as well as covering areas such as the changing role of women; the regeneration of Britain and the impact of migration. They should help children to understand the impact of World War II on their lives today.

WWII is a sensitive issue and activities such as evacuation can provoke emotional responses from children and this will need to be taken in to account before embarking on any of these activities.

WHAT WAS LIFE LIKE IN WORLD WAR II?

A little bit of knowledge . . .

The early part of the twentieth century was a difficult one for Britain; World War I (1914–1918) had left Britain struggling to rebuild itself and the 1930s saw Britain fall into an economic slump. Before the country had managed to recover Britain found itself engaged in war yet again in 1939 with Germany.

World War II was a global war that involved the majority of the world's nations including the great powers. So only 20 years after the end of The Great War (WWI) Britain's men were again sent abroad to fight for their country.

Key vocabulary

Allies, evacuation, battle, Germany, Hitler, land army, propaganda, rations

Life in Britain during the war

Life in Britain changed during the war. The impact of these changes depended on where in Britain you lived: rural or urban areas. Britain was known as the home front which was a way to enable the country to feel as though everyone could contribute to the success of the troops even if they were not fighting on the front line.

Activities

1. Rationing

Before the war much of the food eaten in Britain was imported. When war broke out, enemy ships would prevent trade ships from entering British waters which contributed to a change in diet and the introduction of rationing. Look at the rationing allocation and compare a daily diet in WWII times with the diet they have today. This could link to a healthy eating topic – which diet was the healthiest?

Margarine: 100g	Bacon and ham: 100g	Butter: 50g
Cheese: 50g	Meat: To the value of 1s.2d (6p)	Milk: 3 pints
Sugar: 225g	Eggs: 1 fresh egg a week	Tea: 50g
Jam: 450g every two months	Dried eggs 1 packet every four weeks	Sweets: 350g every four weeks

Look at advertising campaigns that encouraged families to use their leftovers wisely and think about how much food we waste today. Dig for Victory and The Kitchen Front were key campaigns linked to reducing waste.

What was the government aiming to do by producing these posters? How effective do you think these would have been? Explain that these posters such as these were called propaganda posters and were to let people know that they were contributing to the war effort but also to send out a positive message and remind people of the purpose.

2. *Make do and mend*

Look at the Make do and Mend campaign posters before the children create their own project.

Ask children to bring in an item of clothing that they have grown out of or no longer wear and use this to make something that they could sell to raise money for school funds for example: puppets, drawstring purse, bags, cushions, embroidered items.

3. *Following a wartime recipe*

Look at a wartime recipe. Ask pupils to follow the recipe using wartime ingredients if you can source them such as powdered milk and egg.

Eve's pudding

- 6 oz flour or 3 oz flour and 2 oz fine oatmeal or mashed potato
- 3 oz fat
- 2½ oz sugar
- ¼–½ pint milk (powdered or fresh)
- 1 egg (dried or fresh)
- 1 tea-spoon baking powder
- 1 lb jam

Cream the fat and sugar thoroughly. Add the egg, milk and flour in turn, beating all the time. Add the baking powder with the last of the flour. Place the jam carefully at the bottom of the pie dish, cover with the cake mixture and bake in a moderate oven 30–40 minutes.

Explain to the children that as you will, more than likely, be using fresh egg and milk that this will alter the taste and therefore affect the validity of this recipe as a source of evidence. However, if youare able to source powdered milk and egg it may be a good idea to make two different dishes and discuss the differences in taste.

4. *Propaganda posters*

Look at propaganda posters from WWII. Look at German and British posters in order to demonstrate to the children that they were produced on both sides of the war.

Ask pupils to design their own propaganda poster based on a wartime agenda such as saving resources, reusing and recycling or the role of women.

5. *Newspapers and radio broadcasts*

Look at a significant event in WWII such as the beginning of war, the Blitz or D-Day landings. Listen to the radio broadcast and look at newspapers about the event. Discuss the importance of radio at this time in communicating information to the masses – people would often go to neighbours' homes to hear an important broadcast and sales of radios rose during the war as people were keen to know what the latest events were. Pupils can make their own radio broadcast or write a newspaper article about a chosen event using appropriate language and vocabulary.

What was evacuation?

During WWII many children living in urban areas were moved out of the cities to live with foster families (called host families) in the country to keep them safe. They would often be away from their parents for months and years on end. Evacuation began in September 1939 when it became too dangerous to live in the cities; children were allowed to take one small bag with them and would be waved off at the train station by their parents before embarking on their journey. Each child had a small tag which identified who they were, where they'd come from and where they were going.

Activities

1. *Evacuation: packing a suitcase*

Ask pupils to imagine that they are being evacuated and are allowed a small suitcase to take with them – what would they choose and why? As the teacher, model the types of things that evacuees would have had to take and bring in some clothes for the children to select.

Examples of suggested items for evacuees from the Government Evacuation Scheme

Clothing:

- overcoat or mackintosh
- 1 vest
- 1 pair of knickers
- 2 pairs of socks
- 1 pair of trousers
- handkerchiefs
- 1 pullover or jersey

- nightwear
- comb, towel, soap, face-cloth, tooth-brush
- boots or shoes, plimsolls.

Food for the journey:

- sandwiches
- packets of nuts or raisins
- dry biscuits
- barley sugar (rather than chocolate)
- fruit.

Essential items:

- gas masks
- ration books.

This is even more effective if children bring the items from home and take photographs of their suitcases/bags. Discuss what personal items (teddy, treasured toy) they may also take – how does this differ from wartime items?

2. *Sources of evidence*
Look at extracts from a variety of sources to build up a picture of what it must have been like to be an evacuee. Look at the sources provided below and think about the process of evacuation from different points of view. Children could collate their thoughts on a grid:

Person	Viewpoint
Evacuee (child)	
Mother of an evacuated child or children	
Pregnant mother	
Host family's mother	
Host family's children	
Government	
Billeting officers	
Now consider (using the sources and your own research) what the conflicts and issues were with the evacuation scheme	

An extract from *Carrie's War* by Nina Bawden (1973)

Miss Evans looked down at their feet. 'Better change into your slippers before I take you to your bedroom.'

'We haven't any,' Carrie said. She meant to explain that there hadn't been room in their cases for their slippers, but before she could speak Miss Evans turned bright red and said quickly, 'Oh, I'm sorry, how silly of me, why should you have slippers? Never mind as long as you're careful and keep to the middle of the stair carpet where it's covered with a cloth.'

Her brother Nick whispered, 'She thinks we're poor children, too poor to have slippers,' and they giggled.

Quote from a host mother (name unknown)

'I just won't have this child any longer. He wets the bed every night. He was alright at first but now he is awful and do you know what he says to me? He says that he will go on piddling in his bed until he is allowed to go home to his mother again.'

Letter writing

Linking back to their evacuee activity, ask pupils to write a letter as if they were an evacuee or even as if they were a parent. What would they include in their letter? Remind children that although parents missed their children and wanted them home it was not safe so they would be unlikely to say this. Would the letter be upbeat to make the other person feel better? Remind pupils that letters would have been relatively infrequent too.

What does 'World War' mean?

WWII was a global war that involved nearly all parts of the world between 1939 and 1945. The world was divided into the allies (friends) and the axis (enemies). Allies of Great Britain were France, United States, The Soviet Union (later in the war) and the axis was Germany, Italy and Japan.

Activities

1. *A global war*

Look at countries on a world map that would have been used in 1940 (explain to children that this is key as some countries have been renamed since then and borders have changed). Colour code the map into allies and the axis and use this to generate a discussion about why countries forged allegiances and why they changed. It is also important to mention that some countries were neutral and chose not to become involved in the war – why do they think this was?

Allocate a country to each child and ask them to find out key information about their country to share with the class.

Name of country	
Date it became involved in the war	
Who were its allies?	
Who was its leader?	

Use this as an opportunity to demonstrate that whilst we may believe that Germany was the enemy, people living in Germany believed that we were their enemies and that perception and understanding is key. Children to draw the flag of their country on the reverse of the information card above and make a timeline (use a washing line and pegs) to show when countries became involved in the war.

2. *Timeline of the war*

To promote their understanding of chronology, children could sequence the significant events in World War II on a timeline.

1939	• Poland is invaded by German troops • Britain and France declare war on Germany • Evacuation of children out of British cities begins
1940	• The introduction of rationing in UK • Churchill becomes prime minister • Evacuation from Dunkirk • Battle of Britain
1941	• Hitler invades Russia • Japan attacks Pearl Harbour • USA joins the war • Blitz continues and British cities are hit hard

1942	• Mass murder of Jewish people at Auschwitz begins • Singapore is taken over by the Japanese • Battles at El Alamein and Stalingrad see Germany suffer setbacks
1943	• British and Indian forces fight Japanese in Burma • Surrender at Stalingrad marks a major defeat for Germany • Italy is invaded and surrenders
1944	• D-Day – The Allied invasion of France. Paris is liberated • Soviet forces begin to dominate Eastern Europe
1945	• Atomic bombs are dropped on Hiroshima and Nagasaki – Japan surrenders • Auschwitz is liberated by Soviet troops • Russians invade Berlin • Hitler commits suicide and Germany surrenders

This is an opportunity to explore some specific questions to encourage children's enquiry skills.

1. What year do you think it started to go wrong for Germany? Children could write an extended piece of writing on what year and what event was the tipping point for Germany.
2. What was the most significant event and/or which event has had the most impact on our lives today? You could encourage the children to discuss the significance of the use of atomic bombs – was it successful? How has this impacted on warfare today?
3. Would the mass genocide of Jewish people happen today? Discuss with children the many millions of people who were killed in the war – how did this happen? How was Hitler able to justify this? (You could look back at some of the propaganda posters highlighting the Jews as being at the root of Germany's economic difficulties).

4. Children could look at the impact of events in the war on our lives today by focusing on Remembrance Day – what does it signify? Why is it important to look back at battles and events from many years ago?
5. Focus on Hitler by discussing with the children his journey to power. Consider what qualities Hitler must have had in order to be able to make people follow him, for example: he must have been a good leader as well as having other factors on his side such as the aftermath of WWI and poverty and economic crisis in Germany – people were ready for a strong leader to guide them.

Some significant people in the war

There were many significant people in the war and world leaders such as Hitler, Stalin, Mussolini, Roosevelt and Churchill became well-known household names. However, there were also other people who played a significant and crucial role in the war who are not so well known today. The activities below aim to provide a balance between key leaders and figures and influential people.

Activities

1. Adolf Hitler

Look at some quotes from Adolf Hitler and use these to begin to answer the question 'What sort of leader was Adolf Hitler?'

The victor will never be asked if he told the truth.	Strength lies not in defence but in attack.
The art of leadership . . . consists in consolidating the attention of the people against a single adversary and taking care that nothing will split up that attention.	If you tell a big enough lie and tell it frequently enough, it will be believed. Make the lie big, make it simple, keep saying it, and eventually they will believe it.

2. *Winston Churchill*

Do the same activity for Churchill – look at quotes and use these to begin to answer the question 'What sort of leader was Winston Churchill?'

You have enemies? Good. That means you have stood up for something, sometime in your life.	You can always count on Americans to do the right thing – after they have tried everything else.
Courage is the first of human qualities because it is the quality that guarantees all the others.	The problems of victory are more agreeable than the problems of defeat but they are no less difficult.

Children could then go on to think about the impact that their leaders would have had on the feelings of the people. Churchill spread the message that it was important to work together against a common enemy and promised victory; Hitler spread the same message but in a different way – get children to think about what that difference was.

3. *Anne Frank*

Provide children with an overview of who Anne Frank was and why she is still remembered today before asking them to think about whether her diary is a good source of evidence and how it can be used to help us understand what life was like for Jewish people in WWII.

Look at how a single candle can both defy and define the darkness.	People can tell you to keep your mouth shut but that doesn't stop you from having your own opinion.

If we bear all this suffering and if there are still Jews left when it is over, then Jews, instead of being doomed will be held up as an example.	Leave me in peace, let me sleep one night at least without my pillow being wet with tears, my eyes burning and my head throbbing.

Looking at the quotes above, discuss what this tells us about her life. How does this help us understand what life was like for persecuted Jews in WWII?

4. *Dame Vera Lynn*

Look at some titles and lyrics from songs that were performed by Dame Vera Lynn. What clues do these provide about her role in the war and the meaning and message behind the songs? She used to entertain the troops and raise their spirits during the conflicts and many people left at home, missing their loved ones would listen to her music as a source of comfort. She was known as the 'forces sweetheart' and is still held in high esteem by veterans and the armed forces today.

Song titles:

- *We'll Meet Again*
- *The White Cliffs of Dover*
- *A Nightingale Sang in Berkeley Square*
- *There'll Always Be an England*
- *Auf Wiederseh'n Sweetheart*
- *My Son, My Son*

Lyrics for *We'll Meet Again*.

> We'll meet again,
> Don't know where, don't know when,
> But I know we'll meet again, some sunny day.
> Keep smiling through,
> Just like you always do,
> Till the blue skies drive the dark clouds, far away.

So will you please say hello,
To the folks that I know,
Tell them I won't be long, (I won't be long)
They'll be happy to know that as you saw me go
I was singing this song.

We'll meet again,
Don't know where, don't know when,
But I know we'll meet again, some sunny day.
We'll meet again,
Don't know where, don't know when,
But I know we'll meet again, some sunny day.
Keep smiling through,
Just like you always do,
Till the blue skies drive the dark clouds, far away.

5. Noor Inayat Khan

Provide the children with information about Noor Inayat Khan before setting them a discussion question.

Noor Inayat Khan was a descendant of Tipu Sultan who was a well known ruler of India in the eighteenth century and was raised by her father who was a Sufi preacher and a musician. Noor began to write stories for children and had her first book published in 1939 called *20 Jakarta Tales*. When war broke out Noor decided that although her religion (Sufi) preached non-violence she could not stand by and watch it happen therefore she moved to London and joined the Women's Auxiliary Air Force. When Special Forces operatives were recruiting members Noor was selected as she was a trained radio operator and could speak fluent French. This led to Noor Inayat Khan becoming a wartime British spy. She knew the risks as she had been told she would be shot if caught but still went ahead. She was sent in to Nazi occupied France but was arrested and eventually executed by the Gestapo. However, she never revealed any of British intelligence and was posthumously awarded the George cross for her duties in 1949.

After sharing the information above with the children ask them to discuss the following question:

Should Noor Inayat Khan be remembered and honoured?

Ask children to think about reasons why she should be remembered and reasons why she should not. They should justify their reasons and form a balanced argument (this could be written down or discussed). Ask children to think about how we remember significant people (statues, films, art, awards named after them, medals, buildings or objects named after them). Which do they think would be fitting for Noor and why? You can share with the children that there is a statue of her in Gordon Square in London and that she has a memorial trust in her name.

6. Edward Yeo-Thomas

Forest Frederick Edward Yeo-Thomas was a spy who worked for the British Royal Air Force in the war and is often thought to have been the inspiration for Ian Fleming's James Bond character.

Rather than provide the children with information; put them into groups and give each group a different source of information. They can then make a mind map using their source as a stimulus before swapping sources and adding to their mind map. They should do this with all of the sources to help them build up a picture of Edward Yeo-Thomas and his life.

You could also include an image of Edward Yeo-Thomas as an additional source.

Using their mind maps to support them ask children to answer the following questions:

- Who was Edward Yeo-Thomas?
- Should he be remembered and why?
- How should we remember him?

When children have done the activities above they can then choose one significant person that they would like to research in more depth. These could then be used in a number of different ways:

Source 1: An extract from a letter written by Edward Yeo-Thomas to his commanding officer

My dear Dizzy,

These are 'famous last words' I am afraid, but one has to face death one day or another so I will not moan and get down to brass tacks.

I will not attempt to make a report on my journey except to say that up to the very moment of my arrest it had been a success and I had got things cracking and woken up a number of slumberers. I was quite pleased with things – I took every precaution and neglected nothing – my capture was due to one of those incidents one cannot provide for – I had so much work that I was overwhelmed so I asked . . . to provide me with a sure dependable agent de liaison, and he gave me a young chap called Guy, whom I renamed Antonin. He worked for me for a week, and then got caught; how I do not know, but in any case, he had an appointment with me at 11 a.m. on Tuesday 21st March at the . . . and brought the Gestapo with him. He was obviously unable to withstand bullying and very quickly gave in to questioning. I was caught coming round a corner and had not an earthly chance, being collared and handcuffed before I could say 'knife'. I was badly beaten up in the car on the way to Gestapo H.Q., arriving there with a twisted nose and a head about twice its normal size.

- 'top trumps style' significance cards
- a biography book of significant people
- information cards
- presentations
- podcasts or a web page
- writing in 'the style of' their person to demonstrate their understanding
- hot seating and role play.

Source 2: An extract from a newspaper article about Edward's George Cross Award. Published in the London Gazette on 15 February 1946

The KING has been graciously pleased to award the GEORGE CROSS to:

Acting Wing Commander Forest Frederick Edward YEO-THOMAS, M.C. (39215), Royal Air Force Volunteer Reserve.

This officer was parachuted into France on the 25th February, 1943. He showed much courage and initiative during his mission, particularly when he enabled a French officer who was being followed by a Gestapo agent in Paris to reach safety and resume clandestine work in another area. He also took charge of a U.S. Army Air Corps officer who had been shot down and, speaking no French, was in danger of capture. This officer returned to England on the 15th April, 1943, in the aircraft which picked up Wing Commander Yeo-Thomas.

Wing Commander Yeo-Thomas undertook a second mission on the 17th September, 1943. Soon after his arrival in France many patriots were arrested. Undeterred, he continued his enquiries and obtained information which enabled the desperate situation to be rectified. On six occasions he narrowly escaped arrest. He returned to England on the 15th November, 1943, bringing British intelligence archives which he had secured from a house watched by the Gestapo.

This officer was again parachuted into France in February, 1944. Despite every security precaution he was betrayed to the Gestapo in Paris on the 21st March.......

Wing Commander Yeo-Thomas thus turned his final mission into a success by his determined opposition to the enemy, his strenuous efforts to maintain the morale of his fellow-prisoners and his brilliant escape activities. He endured brutal treatment and torture without flinching and showed the most amazing fortitude and devotion to duty throughout his service abroad, during which he was under the constant threat of death.

Source 3: An account of Edward Yeo-Thomas by his colleague Andre Dewavrin

Edward Yeo-Thomas was one of the most magnificent heroes of the war, a valued comrade, a dear friend, with intelligence and quiet and determined courage.

WHAT WAS LIFE LIKE IN POST-WAR BRITAIN?

World War II had a lasting impact on life in Britain. During the war women had to take on roles that were traditionally held by men such as working in ammunition factories; farming and driving buses. When the men returned home the women were expected to return to the submissive wife and mother role and not all of them were happy with this. Divorce rates peaked as women struggled to find their place in society.

Britain invited many people to come and work in the country from the commonwealth countries in order to help the dwindled population rebuild the cities quickly. These immigrants were often treated differently as some people in Britain struggled to accept the changes that were occurring.

Activities

1. *Migration stories*

After the war there was an influx of people from the commonwealth countries who were drafted in to help rebuild Britain and fill in some of the gaps in the workforce. One of the most famous of these is the Empire Windrush ship which sailed from the Caribbean to Britain on 22 June 1948; many of the passengers had fought in the war alongside British troops and others were simply excited to visit the 'mother country' and sought better opportunities. Ask pupils to imagine they are going to a new country for the first time – what do they think the difficulties would be? How would they overcome these?

Images of migration can be used as a stimulus for this activity.

Extend this initial discussion by asking children to focus on how the mass immigration to Britain would have been viewed by different groups of people . Use the scenarios below to support them in thinking about the thoughts, feelings and behaviours of each group of people.

Young Jamaican man who has returned from the war and has decided to migrate to Britain for a few years.	Young British man who fought in the war and has returned to Britain to rebuild your life.	Young British mother whose husband has returned from the war and is working at the factory where she herself worked during the war.
Young British mother whose husband died in the war. She is struggling to support herself and her young children.	Jamaican teacher who has decided to come and teach in the UK.	A young Jamaican man who was too young to sign up for the forces during the war and has decided to come to the 'mother country' to try and make some money.
A WWI veteran who did not fight in WWII and is struggling to cope with the changes.	A factory owner who needs a large, strong workforce as quickly as possible.	A house owner who is looking to rent rooms to make some money.

2. *The changing role of women*

Give pupils a brief overview of what the role and expectations of women were pre-war (homemakers, caring for husband and children) and then look at how the lives of women have changed and developed since the war. Begin to think about what prompted this and the reasons behind the changes, for example: women were made to fill in the roles that men had previously held when they went to war and found that they could juggle their roles and were no longer content to stay at home; there was also a number of single mothers following the war who needed to work to support their children.

Ask children to do a diamond nine ranking activity. Recreate the cards below and ask the class to sort the cards below twice: once as if they were in 1945 and one from today's perspective.

A woman's place is in the home	Women are better at caring for children than men	Men and women should be treated equally and have equal rights
Women should only have jobs if they have lost their husbands	Women should not be allowed to take the jobs that could be done by men	Women should not have management positions or manage men
Women are better suited to jobs in the caring profession such as nurses, teachers and catering	Men are stronger than women and should have priority over women for manual work	Men should be paid more as it is their job to support their family

CHAPTER 8

Local history

The activities in this chapter provide ways in which children can begin to understand how life in their local area has changed and make comparisons between the way life is for them today and the way it was in the past.

This chapter will provide activities which will help to develop children's understanding of their locality and how it has been shaped by the past.

These activities will include activities such as: using census data; using a variety of sources to begin to ask questions about their local area and having first hand opportunities to investigate a variety of sources including physical artefacts.

Local history activities will require additional planning and resourcing as these will need to be specific to the locality being studied.

WHAT EVIDENCE IS THERE IN MY LOCAL AREA TO HELP ME FIND OUT ABOUT THE PAST?

A little bit of knowledge . . .

Local history allows children to have the opportunity to engage with the physical environment that they live in and use this to begin to ask and answer questions about events that happened in the past. The activities below provide children with the opportunity to draw on the sources around them such as the local library and archives as well as using local knowledge by speaking to members of the community. It also gives them the chance to spend time in their local area; looking at it from different viewpoints and perspectives and opening their eyes to their environment.

Key vocabulary

census, childhood, detectives, primary and secondary sources

In this section the word 'local' is used to describe not only the locality that surrounds the child's house or school but also the locality of familiar locations, for example: grandparents' houses; frequently visited areas such as beaches or cities. This can also mean places where children have a connection, for example: if a child's family is originally from Poland then they may have a connection with a locality in another country that they know well and can draw upon to enhance their historical enquiry skills. It is important when studying local history that the studies are real and relevant to the child as an individual.

Activities

1. *History detectives*

Take children for a walk down your local high street and ask them to look for clues that may help them work out how the high street has developed over time. Look up, look down, look all around: can they see signs painted on shops; old dates on buildings; any feature that looks out of place that may indicate development of that building or those around it. Ask children to take photographs of what they see to look at back in the classroom. Compare the photos you have taken of the high street with old photographs – use this to form enquiry questions and begin to discover how the high street has changed and developed over time.

Enquiry questions:

- What evidence of the past have I seen?
- What changes can I identify using the sources I have?
- Why did these changes happen and when?
- How have changes impacted on the lives of people in my area?

2. Ask an expert

Get in touch with your local historical association or a local history group in your area. Invite a guest speaker in to provide an oral account of the local area. Children can ask questions based on what they already know. Following the visit ask the children to think about the validity of the account they heard. How reliable is oral history as a source of evidence? Ask them to find other evidence to support the historical recount; use the grid below to structure children's collection of evidence.

What do I already know about my local area?
What would I like to find out? (Questions)
What did I learn from the visitor's account that I did not already know?
What else do I need to find to support the evidence I have?
What do I still need to find out?

3. *Using census data*

Get the census data for your local area and identify a street in the locality. Using the census data, allocate children roles within family groups that lived in the street. From this, children can begin to build a picture of what life was like in their area in the past using their inference skills and factual information they may have found from other sources. This will enable them to create a realistic interpretation of life in the past. Use drama and role play to encourage empathy and give children the opportunity to act out realistic scenarios and situations that may have taken place, for example: taking in a lodger to get more money for the family; preparing a family meal for when the husband returned from work; distributing wages at the end of the week. The role play will obviously be dependent on the history of the area and roles will need to be allocated according the jobs and professions outlined on the census report.

4. *Using primary and secondary sources of information*

It is important for children to question the reliability of the sources they use in their investigations. Provide children with a series of questions that they can use to make judgements on reliability of sources such as:

- Who wrote this?
- How do they know the information?
- Why was it written?
- Who was it written for?
- When was it written – at the time or at a later date?

Encourage the children to look at a range of primary and secondary sources such as:

- primary: autobiographies, official documents, diaries, eye witness accounts, film footage, newspaper articles, artefacts from the time, photographs, laws
- secondary: biographies, encyclopaedias, text books, films or novels, replicas.

5. *Freeze frame*

Find a picture from the local area which shows people involved in day-to-day activities from the past. Following discussion, ask children to create a montage (freeze-frame) of the image. The rest of the class can 'unfreeze' a child and ask them questions about their character. They are to respond in role. Ensure that you spend plenty of time discussing questions and answers prior to this activity so that children feel they have enough information to respond in character. This will encourage the children to develop their empathy skills and understand what life may have been like in the past.

6. *Solving a mystery!*

Tell the children that they are history detectives looking at sources of information to find out the truth.

- Provide two different newspaper articles about the same event but from different perspectives and ask children to look for facts, interpretations and opinions.
- Provide two letters or oral accounts from two different people involved in the same event but with different accounts and ask pupils to think about why they are different – how is it that two people who have experienced the same thing will have different perspectives? What does this tell us about the validity of sources?

The children have to use primary and secondary sources of evidence to find out which account is correct. This would be a good opportunity to ask grandparents or older members of the community to come and share their experiences of life in the local area and their memories of key events or time periods in the past.

7. *What is local to me?*

Get children to make a mind map (individually) of places and people that are important to them, and look for connections and shared experiences with members of the class. Explain that local history may not just be the area around their school but could be much wider.

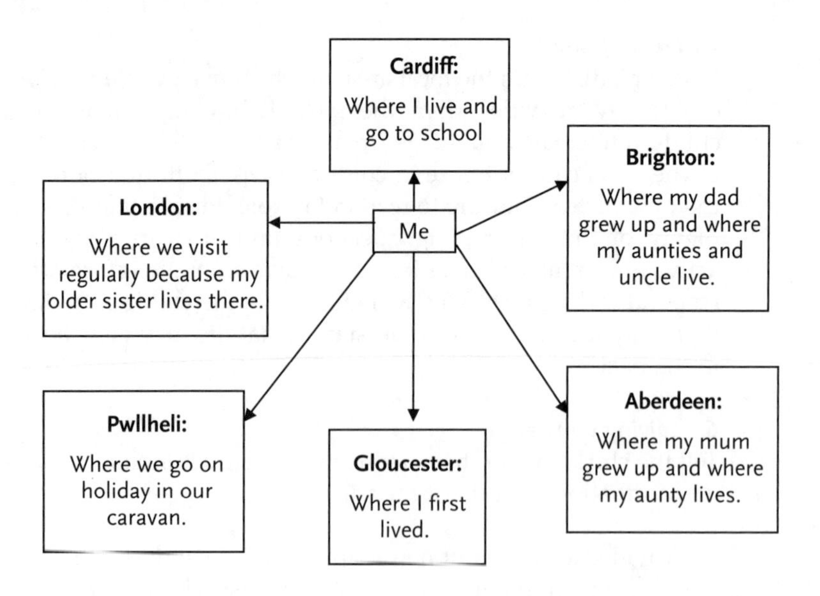
Cardiff:
Where I live and go to school
London:
Where we visit regularly because my older sister lives there.
Me
Brighton:
Where my dad grew up and where my aunties and uncle live.
Pwllheli:
Where we go on holiday in our caravan.
Gloucester:
Where I first lived.
Aberdeen:
Where my mum grew up and where my aunty lives.

Concluding comments

We hope that you now feel able to develop the ideas in this book further by conducting your own research with the children and developing the historical skills of:

- enquiry
- identifying significance
- chronology
- interpretation and historical understanding
- understanding cause and consequence
- recognising change and continuity.